MARKETING

LILA STAIR AND LESLIE STAIR

FOURTH EDITION

New York Chicago San Francisco Lisbon London Madrid Mexico City
Milan New Delhi San Juan Seoul Singapore Sydney Toronto

The McGraw·Hill Companies

1 2 3 4 5 6 7 8 9 10 11 12 13 14 15 16 17 18 19 20 21 DOC/DOC 0 9 8

ISBN 978-0-07-149312-3
MHID 0-07-149312-3

McGraw-Hill books are available at special quantity discounts to use as premiums and sales promotions or for use in corporate training programs. To contact a representative, please visit the Contact Us pages at www.mhprofessional.com.

This book is printed on acid-free paper.

To Terri, our favorite plethora of knowledge.
To Tony, Ryan, John, and Grant for making a wonderful internship experience possible.

CONTENTS

PREFACE

Marketing, in its simplest form, began in the earliest times of barter and trade, often carried out, no doubt, even without a common language. Goods for exchange between just two or a few people—perhaps shells, bones, furs, grain, slaves, or tools—would be laid out, and their appeal would be made clear with sign language, gestures, and expressions. The purpose was to get the goods exchanged and to get the best deal possible.

Later, with language, with villages, and with crossroads, the first marketplaces were established, and larger groups of people could use expanded methods to market their goods. As specialization increased in societies, more services could be bartered or sold as well. Marketing methods increased to talking, singing, chanting, and calling out about the goods and services for sale. The goal remained the same: to get the best possible return for the goods and services being bartered and sold.

In that basic purpose, not much has changed. Marketing is still involved with presentation of goods and services for exchange or sale, and with getting the best possible deal. The goods and services for sale—the products—and the methods of marketing have become almost incredibly more complex.

Billions of products, customers, and sales and marketing workers and a nearly infinite torrent of words and images now fill the global marketplace every hour of every day on planet Earth. The field of marketing offers countless professional opportunities for businesspeople, salespersons, writers, artists, mathematicians, and planners. Among these, advertising, marketing, and public relations managers, management analysts, and college and university professors represent the fastest-growing occupations.

Choosing a college major that leads to a satisfying career is not easy. The choices are many and varied. Often students opt for college majors based on academic aptitudes, a single strong interest, personal values, or market factors, which sometimes change. Experiencing the work itself as early as possible through part-time jobs and internships will help individuals realize whether their career choices are wise ones for them.

Marketing professionals are employed in every type of industry and nonprofit organization, including government. Employment with large advertising, sales promotion, public relations, and consulting agencies offers the possibility of advancement to partner, enabling an individual to share proportionately in the profits of the agency. Marketing fields also offer numerous options for self-employment as manufacturers' agents, entrepreneurs, and consultants in such areas as marketing strategy, public relations, and advertising. Whatever an individual's interests and values, marketing has something to offer.

Career decision making is complex. It requires a careful analysis of one's strengths and weaknesses, and it has a major impact on one's quality of life and the achievement of personal goals. A career decision-making model that incorporates both internal and external factors affecting career choice follows. It was developed to enable individuals to better evaluate the career options discussed in this book. The blank lines in the model enable career decision makers to add factors important to them and to rank the factors in terms of their relative importance.

Among the factors influencing an individual's career choice are careers of family members, guidance from teachers, suggestions from friends, personal interests, and values. A college education requires a large commitment of time, money, and energy, and selecting a college major demands careful consideration. Even students who have already chosen a college major should explore other options early in their education to be sure that they have chosen wisely. Some students become dissatisfied with their original choice when they begin to take courses in the field, and they find they want to change majors. Advisers assigned to students can provide some help in career exploration, but many are specialists in their subject areas or in a general counseling area and are not career specialists. It is important to ask for the specific kind of adviser that you need for your particular situation.

Internal factors	External factors
Aptitudes and attributes	Family influence
____ Academic aptitudes and achievement	____ Family values and expectations
____ Occupational aptitudes and skills	____ Socioeconomic level
____ Social skills	____ ________
____ Communication skills	____ ________
____ Leadership abilities	____ ________
____ ________	____ ________
____ ________	____ ________
____ ________	____ ________
Interests	Economic influence
____ Amount of supervision	____ Overall economic conditions
____ Amount of pressure	____ Employment trends
____ Amount of variety	____ Job market information
____ Amount of work with data	____ ________
____ Amount of work with people	____ ________
____ ________	____ ________
____ ________	____ ________
____ ________	____ ________
____ ________	____ ________
Values	Societal influence
____ Salary	____ Perceived effect of race, sex, or ethnic background on success
____ Status/prestige	____ Perceived effect of physical or psychological handicaps on success
____ Advancement opportunity	
____ Growth on the job	
____ ________	____ ________
____ ________	____ ________
____ ________	____ ________
____ ________	____ ________
____ ________	____ ________
____ ________	____ ________

Today, most college campuses have career information centers available both to students and to members of the community who are interested in exploring career options. User-friendly computerized career information systems are available in many college career centers. These systems aid students in making career choices by relating responses on a questionnaire to various careers and generating a list of career options based on the responses. Students can then obtain descriptions of careers that look interesting. Many computerized systems provide information on colleges and financial aid as well. Career centers house an array of printed career information, including occupational briefs, current articles, and books such as *Careers in Marketing,* Fourth Edition.

It is our hope that all who explore marketing careers through this book will gain the insights and enthusiasm for marketing that we have gained in writing it. In addition to job descriptions, this book includes personal and educational requirements for those entering marketing careers, salary data, job market information, trends, job search tips, and many sources of further information. Challenges and rewards abound for those entering the field of marketing.

On joining the labor force, the first challenge is to prepare and market oneself. It is the objective of this book to help readers meet that challenge with interest, confidence, and success.

ACKNOWLEDGMENT

The authors wish to thank Barbara Wood Donner for her research and help in preparing the current edition of this book.

CHAPTER 1

MARKETING CAREERS IN THE TWENTY-FIRST CENTURY

Electronic communication has caused a marketing revolution in just the last couple of decades. The influence of computers and the Internet and the rapid spread of a global consumer economy have infused the marketing world with a new excitement and a new, breakneck pace. The effects of the instantaneous cyberspeed of the Internet, e-mail, mobile phones, and texting have blown the lid off the old limits. This new era has made the famously hectic-paced Madison Avenue Hollywood movies of the 1940s and '50s look almost staid by comparison.

Of course, there are still some gentler and slower-paced marketing jobs to be had—some of them are in small towns, with nonprofit organizations, on small newspaper staffs, or in small advertising offices where most of the ads are placed in local hard-copy publications. In general, however, marketers in the twenty-first century had better know state-of-the-art computer science and keep up with all forms of electronic and digital communication if they want to be competitive and successful.

In this world, our national and international computer connections with each other play a significant role in every aspect of our lives, impacting the way we live, play, work, and learn. E-commerce is affecting how we become aware of new products, what products we buy, and the ways in which we buy them.

THE INTERNET REVOLUTION

By 2005, the number of Internet users in the United States was estimated to be 1,018,057,389, according to the *World Fact Book*, published by the United States Central Intelligence Agency (CIA). And the technology is spreading everywhere. In China, users already totaled 132 million in 2006, according to the Xinhua News Agency. An incredible number of websites have been developed to provide these Internet users with information and products in every conceivable area, including health, travel, job placement, and investment. It is not surprising, therefore, that the Internet economy now plays a surpassingly important part in nearly all marketing careers.

The Internet economy is supporting the growth of new companies that are offering a wide variety of products—new and old—online. Many online resources provide marketing professionals with amazingly detailed data on consumers and also with ways to improve every aspect of the marketing process.

Changing demographics are also significantly impacting the types of products being offered, the number and kinds of sales opportunities, and, ultimately, the number of available jobs for many kinds of workers. In developed countries, people are continuing to live longer, with a growing number of them aged sixty-five and over. Many in this group may also be caring for elderly parents and may have to work for salaries and wages beyond the traditional retirement age. Having children later in life affects the level of affluence in many families, and people may therefore be able to afford more consumer products for their children.

Marketers must take into consideration everything that impacts the kind and quantity of products that are to be produced and the numbers of qualified workers that are available to produce and sell those products.

No field in business offers a greater variety of career choices than marketing. Challenges in the field abound as marketers grapple with emerging markets, technology, changing demographics, economies in flux, changing tastes and values, emerging and disappearing brands, and numerous other factors that affect marketing decisions.

Consumers are bombarded with information about product offerings from thousands of companies of all sizes, not only in the United States but also in neighboring countries in the Americas and farther away in Africa, Asia, Europe, and the South Pacific. In addition, these companies offer far more than just new products; they also offer business and career opportunities for North American companies to collaborate in business ventures and for Americans who want to work abroad.

EVOLUTION OF THE FIELD OF MARKETING

Marketing, as a human activity, has been around since primitive people began to barter and exchange goods that were plentiful for those that were scarce. They traded tools, grain, meat, jewelry, hides, animals, and human slaves, among other things.

The concept of trade already existed in prehistoric times and was not so different from what it is today. The board of directors of the American Marketing Association (AMA) has defined marketing as

> the process of planning and executing the conception, pricing, promotion, and distribution of ideas, goods, and services to create exchanges that satisfy individual and organizational objectives.

The concept of a "product" today encompasses ideas and services as well as goods. As the AMA definition suggests, marketing professionals are involved in every stage of the formation of a product—from its conception to its actual sale and sometimes its distribution.

The Production Era. The field of marketing has evolved over many centuries. Early European settlers in North America hunted, fished, and farmed to attain what they needed to survive. Gradually they were able to produce a little surplus and traded with other settlers and explorers and with Native Americans. The growth of settlements encouraged trade as well—the colonists playing an active role in the "production era" of marketing that lasted in the Western world for roughly three hundred years.

During those years, production evolved into a custom process that provided consumers with many goods of value for which they would exchange other goods, gold, or money. Initially, many of the more processed products, such as saddles, fine furniture, ceramics, and silver pieces, were produced only on customer demand. By the 1800s, however, larger producers were beginning to anticipate and plan on consumer demand and were creating an increasing inventory of products ahead of time.

Mass Production. The Industrial Revolution was in full swing by the second half of the nineteenth century, and mass production of many consumer products had become commonplace, especially in urban areas of the United States and Canada. Unlike in the early part of the century, when small quantities were produced and customers were geographically close to producers, by 1850, mass production created the need for new sales and distribution strategies. Trains, coaches, and river travel developed, allowing for more effective shipment of larger quantities of goods farther from their sources of production.

The Sales Era. Thus, the "traveling salesman" became a feature of the American landscape as marketing entered its "sales era." Improvements in printing spurred the advent of well-illustrated sales catalogs. "Novelty advertising" companies imprinted their messages on toys, matchboxes, key cases, calendars, toy banks, celluloid collar and collar-button boxes, mustache cups, pocket combs, and myriad other small consumer giveaways to advertise and market their goods. Businesses, such as barbershops, soda fountains, and saloons, received larger novelties, such as Gibson girl posters, brightly silk-screened Coca-Cola trays, and whole cast-iron replicas of beer wagons being pulled by teams of dray horses, which proud saloon keepers displayed above their bars. The creation of "advertising novelties" became a thriving business because it helped to market products faster and to more customers.

Because producers began to have more products to sell than they had customers, they turned their attention to even more persuasive advertising and sales techniques. The "hard sell" was born, and it was widely used, to the fullest extent that consumerism allowed.

Many people think of consumerism as a fairly recent phenomenon, but it actually began in the early 1900s and grew more prevalent as the twentieth century progressed. Legislation regulating both product quality and truth in advertising was enacted prior to World War II. During the war, many consumer products were scarce, and people were happy to get what they could. By the 1950s, however, the U.S. economy was booming, and products were again plentiful. It was at this time that the Marketing Era began.

The Marketing Era. The "marketing era" was characterized by a shift from the previous *sales* orientation to a *market* orientation. Today, the primary emphasis is no longer on selling already planned and produced goods, but rather on identifying customer wants and needs and then planning products specifically to satisfy those demands.

The marketing concept is a philosophy that focuses on customer wants and on clearly identified markets. Companies have found that they can create the desire for certain types of products in well-defined groups of potential customers. In following that model, marketing has become a driving force in the modern consumer society.

Marketing specialists have come from all kinds of backgrounds into this highly charged field, from sales, teaching, and psychology, as well as from the business schools and giant corporations. Powerful trendsetting leaders in major corporations created methods and courses to inspire and develop marketing professionals for the new approach—from manufacturing, the communications industry, and many more areas. Thus, marketing has grown into a vastly complex and sophisticated field, needing a large number of highly trained professionals to perform its many specialized functions.

More Than 750,000 Strong. The American Marketing Association (AMA) has a roster of thirty-eight thousand members and more than seventy-five local and regional chapters, eleven of which are in Canada. It maintains two hundred and fifty student chapters on college campuses in the United States and Canada and is an acknowledged leader in the field, providing professional services in information, education, publications, standards, certification, networking, and career planning. The AMA states that there are more than 750,000 people employed in the various facets of the marketing industry in the United States and Canada today.

SCOPE OF THE MARKETING FIELD

The dramatic evolution of the marketing era increased marketing's functions from advertising and selling, which dominated the sales era, to include market research, product development, packaging, promotion, and public relations.

Marketing begins with the identification of the need for a product, which can be a good or a service, by a particular market. Marketing research specialists perform this job. Marketing researchers locate potential consumer groups, describe the groups in detail, find out what these consumers want, consider these wants in terms of specific products, determine if such products exist and which competing companies are supplying them, and forecast what products consumers are likely to buy in the future and which competitors are likely to produce them. And that's only part of it!

Once a product is conceived, the idea is turned over to product development. Professionals under the direction of a product manager then plan the product in detail. This planning doesn't end with the product itself but encompasses its price, packaging, and distribution. Product management is also involved in all other marketing functions. Additional information may be required from marketing research throughout the planning phase, and ideas for promoting the product may come directly from the product specialists.

There are three major ways to promote a product: advertising, personal selling, and sales promotion.

- **Advertising.** A nonpersonal presentation that uses a variety of media, such as television, radio, newspapers, magazines, handbills, billboards, the Internet, and mobile phones.
- **Personal Selling.** Involves direct customer contact.
- **Sales Promotion.** A concept born of the marketing era, involves three types of product promotion: consumer promotion, trade promotion, and sales force promotion.

Public relations (PR) is a completely separate function from advertising and sales promotion. Public relations specialists work to project a positive company image and to create goodwill with the public. Consumer watchdog groups regularly use public relations to call attention to business practices with which they don't agree. For example, the tuna company that kills dolphins earns the ill will of environmentalists and others who hold dolphins in high regard. Environmentalists monitor the effects on the environment of both products and production processes, and they publicize the results using public relations skills. Manufacturers must, in turn, mount public relations campaigns to counter charges made against them and continually work to maintain a good public image.

Green marketing has been used as a strategy for many years. Rising interest in eco-friendly cars has caused manufacturers in North America,

China, Europe, India, Japan, and other areas to begin introduction of cars using fuel-efficient, gasoline-electric power trains, smaller size, and other more environment-friendly modifications into the market.

Cause marketing has become increasingly popular with the growth of Internet use. For example, Pura Vida Coffee, created by John Sage, a retired Microsoft executive, and Chris Dearnley, a pastor in Costa Rica, was established to donate its net profits to a locally run ministry and to social programs to help Costa Rican children and families in need. Another example is Yahoo! Auctions, a large, globally branded, free auction site on the Internet, which auctioned off autographed jeans donated by more than seventy celebrities, with proceeds going to the National Multiple Sclerosis Society's chapter in Southern California. The snowboard manufacturer HardCloud.com sponsored "Boarding for Breast Cancer," a charity snowboarding event to raise money for the Susan G. Komen Foundation, the Nina Hyde Center for Breast Cancer Research, and numerous local organizations. Cause marketing promotes and markets sales to benefit nonprofit organizations and projects, just as marketing would be done for any other product. The cause projects bring good public relations to their sponsors and provide marketers with welcome opportunities to do worthwhile and satisfying work.

Nonprofit organizations such as charities, the arts, educational institutions, and federal and local governments use the marketing concept to promote their causes as well. When a nonprofit organization is soliciting funds or promoting ideas, it functions in much the same way as a business selling goods or services. The expanded scope of marketing in society today accounts for the many jobs available to people with marketing backgrounds.

OVERVIEW OF MARKETING CAREERS

An understanding of the variety of marketing careers can be gleaned by looking at the breadth of the marketing function itself. Several branches of marketing are sketched here. Figure 1.1 shows key management positions and functional areas and how they relate to one another. Corporate marketing management positions are discussed in Chapter 8.

Figure 1.1 Management of Marketing Functions

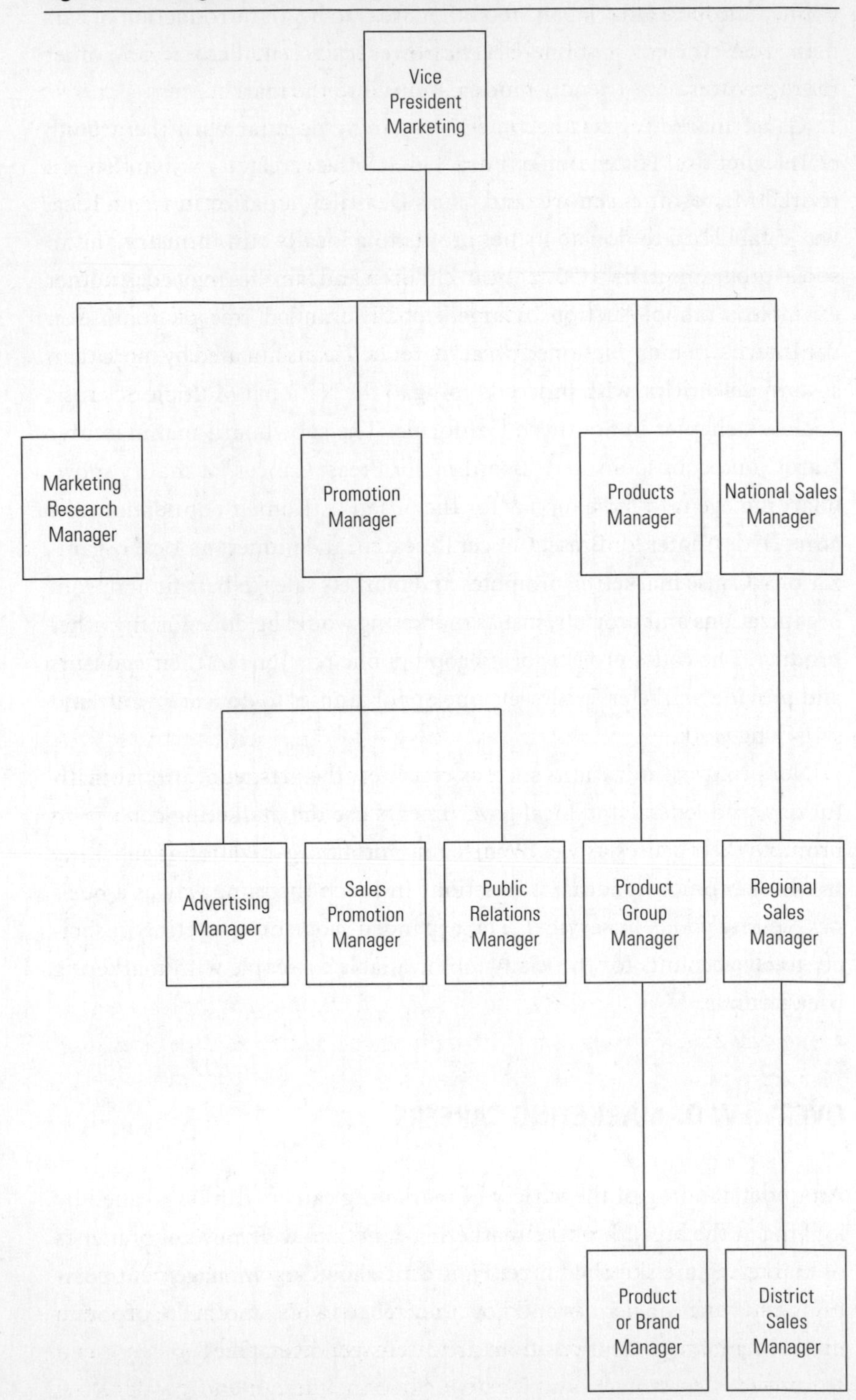

Marketing Research

Approaching the functional areas chronologically in terms of the marketing process, the first major area is marketing research. Manufacturers must learn whether consumers will buy a proposed product before committing substantial time and money to developing it. This is the work of the marketing research department, which includes the director, researcher analysts (researchers), and trainees when it is part of a company. These individuals generally have degrees in marketing, with strong backgrounds in statistics and psychology. Researcher analysts may also work in marketing research firms or as independent consultants. Marketing research is explored in Chapter 2.

Product Development

Once a firm is committed to developing a product, a product manager is assigned or hired to spearhead the project. This position is often entitled "brand manager" in firms producing consumer products. The manager assembles a development team, whose members first work with marketing researchers to further define the characteristics of the product; then they work with engineers in the design and production phases; next they work with the advertising and sales promotion professionals until they finally finish with sales personnel. Members of the product development team are involved in naming, packaging, and distributing the product. They come from different departments throughout the organization and are in a unique position to interact with almost every department in the company. Because product development is so visible, it can be an excellent avenue of advancement to other positions within the company. Chapter 3 details the work of the development team from the inception to the completion of the project.

Advertising

Of all marketing careers, advertising is perhaps the most competitive. Whether employed by a company or an advertising agency, professionals must work in a highly charged atmosphere with extreme pressure to produce. In a company, the advertising manager determines how to spend the advertising budget, and creative personnel design and produce the advertisements. These ads are turned over to media professionals, who plan marketing strategy and buy airtime on television or radio and space in printed media or on the Internet. Research professionals study both consumers' perceptions of products and advertising effectiveness. They also interact with creative and media personnel in the initial production of ads and in subsequent modifications of ad campaigns. For each product, the advertising manager must decide whether to conduct the ad campaign completely in-house or to hire an outside agency. Advertising professionals employed by agencies perform the same functions already described. Usually, advertising agencies have four departments: creative, media, research, and account services. In the account services department, an account executive oversees the ad campaign and serves as the liaison between the agency and the client. Chapter 4 describes an especially wide range of advertising positions, with varying backgrounds and duties.

Sales Promotion

In addition to advertising, sales promotion and public relations campaigns generate sales. These two areas are completely separate and have totally different objectives. Closely linked to advertising, which is a nonpersonal presentation, sales promotion targets the consumer more individually. An industry saying is "Advertising suggests, while sales promotion motivates." Sales promotion falls into three categories:

- **Consumer Promotion.** Includes samples, coupons, rebates, games, contests, and other incentives.
- **Trade Promotion.** For intermediaries such as dealers and distributors, includes cooperative ads, free goods, and dealer sales contests.
- **Sales Force Promotion.** Includes such incentives as sales meetings, contests for prizes, and bonuses.

Specialists in sales promotion usually have some sales or advertising experience. These professionals may be employed by corporate producers or sales promotion agencies, which play a role similar and closely related to that of advertising agencies, as discussed in Chapter 4. Many agencies combine these areas of service, describing themselves as "advertising and sales promotion" agencies.

Public Relations

Both sales promotion and advertising focus on specific products. The sale of all products in a company may be improved through the creation of goodwill. The mission of a public relations department is to build and maintain the company's positive image. Large companies have public relations departments with staffs of specialists who work under a director of public relations. Smaller companies may hire one individual to conduct public relations activities. Some organizations hire public relations agencies that function in the same manner as advertising or sales promotion agencies. Public relations specialists provide information about the organization to news media, arrange speaking engagements for company officials, and usually write the speeches for these engagements. Individuals need not have marketing degrees to enter public relations; in fact, public relations people tend to come from a wide variety of backgrounds. However, they are all involved in selling—selling the organization to the public. Public relations fits easily into the marketing effort of a company, as can be seen in Chapter 5.

Distribution and Sales

The combined efforts of advertising, sales promotion, and public relations professionals create consumer awareness of a company and its products. The producer must then choose how to transport its products from warehouses to the consumers. This process, called distribution, may be done through various channels. Options include the sale of the product to wholesalers, retailers, or directly to the consumer.

Sales and customer service are the keys to running a successful business in today's economy. Professional salespeople are the backbone of any company. Without an effective sales force, a company cannot survive. With so many similar products available in a competitive global environment, it is the sales force that makes the difference. Many marketing graduates start in sales. This area is where beginners can truly learn their company's business and make contributions to profits. It is an opportunity for an individual's hard work to really pay off both in increased earnings and in recognition.

Retail salespeople sell products to the final consumer. Wholesale and industrial sales personnel sell both finished products and basic materials to retailers, other intermediate agents, and manufacturers. Industrial sales representatives are employed by manufacturers, but they are not the only ones selling the company's products. Manufacturers' representatives are independent businesspeople who may sell one or more companies' products to many different customers. Finally, self-employed wholesale dealers find needed products for client companies. Chapters 6 and 7 describe wholesaling and retailing, respectively.

Direct marketing, or nonstore selling, is growing at a faster rate than in-store selling and includes such methods as e-commerce, direct selling, direct response retailing, database marketing, direct mail, and teleservices. Direct marketing offers a variety of career opportunities and is discussed in Chapter 6.

Marketing careers are varied and interesting. Depending on a person's verbal or quantitative strengths, interests, creativity, sales flair, and initiative, one of these careers could be a wise choice and provide opportunities for success.

TRENDS AFFECTING MARKETING CAREERS

Marketing occurs in an ever-changing environment to which marketing professionals must continually adapt. The economy of the 1990s was bolstered by a number of knowledge-driven industries, including computer hardware, computer software, telecommunications, the Internet, film and TV production, financial services, medical research, and tourism. The crash of the IT boom brought a reorganization of many related industries, and the aftermath of the terrorists' attack on September 11, 2001, brought disaster to the U.S. airlines and related travel industries, along with many others. Jobs in all service industries declined as the nation tightened its belt, and many companies had to lay off employees.

Since that time, the monetary, psychological, and other costs of the U.S. invasion and occupation of Iraq, and the long-standing occupation in Afghanistan, along with widely publicized corruption and mistaken judgments in business and finance in the United States, have heavily drained the U.S. economy and weakened the U.S. dollar abroad. The balance of trade has been affected by these changes, and according to some estimates, the U.S. economy may have a period of stagnant or negative growth ahead.

To maintain a balance, the Federal Reserve Board continually monitors economic factors and adjusts interest rates—using the prime rate—to help stabilize the economy.

Major changes have been expected in the U.S. economy following the national election of 2008, and it is hoped that careful fiscal and foreign policy will help to bring about a return to the positive economic signs that would point to a surge in productivity, an increase in highly skilled workers, efficient capital investment, expanding global trade, the shrinking of the U.S. trade deficit, a healthier dollar in comparison with other international currencies, more affordable and useful information technologies, an increase in patent applications, and a rapidly growing Internet economy.

During the 1990s, marketers operated in a highly price-conscious environment in which customers had increasingly greater and more convenient access to information. This is also the case in the 2000s, when millions of consumers have access to nearly unlimited price and product information via the Internet. In this new environment of online and offline competition, customers must be viewed as assets, and customer service is tantamount to retaining those assets. The marketing of both goods and services will focus on value to the customer as well as customer service, which is discussed in detail in Chapter 5.

The markets of the 1970s changed substantially with the introduction of new technologies, the flood of imports, and the deregulation of airlines and other industries. The 1980s became a decade of mergers and acquisitions as organizations attempted to remain profitable or grow through restructuring. This upheaval created opportunities for entrepreneurs who found market niches—small groups of consumers with unfilled needs for specific goods or services. Record numbers of small businesses were created to meet these needs. Throughout the 1980s and 1990s, an entrepreneurial boom occurred. Though the number of new small businesses has been decreasing, small business owners still provide many new jobs in the economy, particularly as e-businesses that are able to grow more rapidly than traditional small businesses. Chapter 10 describes the special opportunities in marketing in this economic arena for entrepreneurs, franchisees, educators, and consultants.

During the 1990s, the North American Free Trade Agreement (NAFTA) and the General Agreement on Tariffs and Trade (GATT) removed many trade barriers in the Americas, Europe, and Asia. The agreements also facilitated economic globalization, especially by large corporations and government-sponsored enterprises. Improvements in network information technology and their impact on our knowledge-based economy have enabled new businesses to compete in the global economy. One example is E-Latin Business (e-latin.com), which provides technological and financial support and guidance to Internet companies wanting to do business in Latin America.

The trend for American companies to outsource manufacturing and service jobs escalated in the early 2000s, with deep effects on the American workforce and jobs in the United States. This trend showed evidence of beginning to slow by 2007, due to gradually increasing labor and other costs in foreign countries, complications of quality control overseas, the decline in the value of the American dollar, and other changes that relate to profitability.

Another trend that has affected the field of marketing in recent years is the growth in minority populations in the United States and Canada, which is contributing to an increasing diversity of the marketplace. The Hispanic American/Latino population is the fastest-growing minority group in the United States today. Companies such as Cingular Wireless, Heineken, Mott's, and Volkswagen have created marketing campaigns for Hispanic/Latino audiences, featuring television commercials and radio spots that reflect Hispanic/Latino values and employ Hispanic/Latino actors. Internet marketing to Hispanics/Latinos will increase rapidly also, as the number of Hispanic/Latino Internet users is expected to rise to more than twenty million by 2010.

Changing lifestyles and values have a profound impact on markets and products. Working women, who control more and more of the wealth, contribute to the success of establishments that offer the convenience of quick shopping with no waiting in lines. Additionally, our more health-conscious public is demanding reduced fat content and lower levels of refined sugar and preservatives in prepared foods, and because of this, new and more healthful products appear daily on grocery shelves.

Marketing professionals are needed in all of these changing and growing businesses, and job opportunities will be open for those with the best skills and market knowledge.

E-COMMERCE AND GLOBAL MARKETING

Opportunities in global marketing are burgeoning as technology makes foreign markets more accessible. Desktop, laptop, and mobile Internet usage is steadily expanding. According to the Mobile Marketing Association (Global), more than 1.3 billion text messages were sent by mobile phones in December 2005, and by March 2006 more than 3.2 billion messages were sent in a single month. This young organization, which is headquartered in the United States, is expanding rapidly and has offices in several continents. It provides international standards and a forum for professional communication. The guidelines for international marketing standards are available on the association's website. It also publishes a newsletter and the *International Journal of Mobile Marketing.* International conventions planned for 2008 included Sao Paulo, London, New York, and San Diego. This association is a source of information for students as well as professionals and is an emerging leader in the global electronic marketplace.

In England, the Search Marketing Association U.K. (sma-uk.org) was founded in 2005. This organization provides a focal point for marketing professionals and companies in the booming field of search engine marketing.

As American business moves abroad, the need for individuals who are familiar with foreign languages and cultures will grow substantially. Those who are prepared to assume a role in global marketing will find excellent career possibilities, which are discussed in Chapter 9.

A CAREER IN MARKETING

A survey of careers in marketing reveals many challenging professions, including high-interest fields such as advertising and marketing research. Marketing attracts large numbers of people with a variety of interests, experience, and educational backgrounds. Of all concentrations open to college business and communications majors, marketing offers the widest range of career choices. Marketing managers at all levels hold positions with considerable power, because the marketing of products directly affects how companies generate revenues. In a study of business students in the United States, the Philippines, and New Zealand, most students chose marketing management as their preferred career path, followed by management consulting, public relations, product management, and international sales.

Interest inventories can help students make more informed career decisions. James Waldroop and Timothy Butler, as the directors of M.B.A. career-development programs at the Harvard Business School, conducted a twelve-year study of Harvard business students and developed the Business Career Interest Inventory (BCII), which identified eight core sets of activities and related them to successful businesspeople. For example, individuals such as advertising executives, brand managers, salespeople, and public relations specialists were found to be interested in both "creative production," involving highly creative activities, and "influence through language and ideas," involving the use of persuasion to exercise influence over others. Successful CEOs and marketing managers shared interests in both "enterprise control," which involves having strategy and decision-making authority and resource control over an operation, and "influence through language and ideas." For entrepreneurs, short-term project managers, new-product developers, and advertising "creatives," it was "creative production" that dominated their interest.

Marketing jobs offer creativity, challenge, and variety. Today, marketing places a greater emphasis on both customer satisfaction and how to best provide services in our service-oriented economy. An investigation of careers in marketing will point out specific areas of opportunity and the broad nature of marketing as a whole. Successful career preparation requires mastering knowledge and skills in a discipline and educating oneself to compete in today's job market. Our exploration of marketing careers begins at the start of the marketing process, with the specialization, skills, and job opportunities of marketing research.

ADDITIONAL SOURCES OF INFORMATION

The following associations provide a rich source of additional information for students and professionals:

American Marketing Association (AMA)
311 S. Wacker Dr., Ste. 5800
Chicago, IL 60606
marketingpower.com

Canadian Marketing Association
1 Concorde Gate, Ste. 607
Don Mills, ON M3C 3N6
Canada
the-cma.org

Mobile Marketing Association (Global)
1670 Broadway, Ste. 850
Denver, CO 80202
mmaglobal.com

Search Marketing Association U.K.
105 St. Peter's St.
St. Albans, Herts AL1 3EJ
United Kingdom
sma-uk.org

CHAPTER 2

CAREERS IN MARKETING RESEARCH

The American Marketing Association has defined marketing research as

> the use of scientific methods to identify and define marketing opportunities and problems, generate, refine, and evaluate marketing actions, monitor marketing performance, and improve our understanding of marketing as a process.

Marketing research (sometimes also called *market research*, especially in the United Kingdom) has grown gradually and has existed as a distinct professional field for more than seventy years. Over that time, it has developed into a sophisticated, complex, and dynamic profession, using scientific methods and procedures and employing planners, researchers, writers, statisticians, analysts, and many other specialists. It continues to evolve to meet the changing needs in our economy.

In the earlier days of the profession, market researchers often used in-person and telephone surveys to gather information. Today, although those kinds of surveys are still used and still provide important information, the immediate access to valuable data and other information via the Internet has substantially impacted the field, enabling researchers to gather and share information much more rapidly and comprehensively than ever before.

Statisticians, econometric forecasters, anthropologists, sociologists, psychologists, consumer behaviorists, economists, and other highly skilled professionals, as well as project directors, planners, writers, telephone and in-person interviewers, call center managers and supervisors, presenters, meeting organizers, website designers, and other specialists are involved in the many tasks of marketing research.

Identifying current and future trends in order to gauge accurately what consumers are buying now and what they will buy in the future is the challenge that faces all marketing researchers.

Remember this: *Perpetual change in the market (the economy) causes a perpetual need for marketing research.*

Predicting the future is tricky business, and mistakes can be costly to producers of goods and services. The scientific approach used today by marketing research provides a relatively reliable means to help minimize new-product failures.

Market researchers must constantly monitor market performance as well as consumer knowledge, attitudes, values, needs, demographics, and all of the many components in modern society that affect what commercial goods and services will be wanted, needed, and purchased—and therefore will be offered to the public. For determining such offerings, market research provides the most extensive, complex, and in-depth information possible regarding what is important in today's society.

In order to stay competitive, businesses must respond quickly and accurately to changes in consumer attitude and demographics when they plan their new products and marketing programs.

The twenty-first century has brought with it some potentially significant new market factors that have been identified in extensive market research studies. Some of these new developments foreshadow major changes in the buying habits of the American consumer and must be addressed in the marketing plans of major corporations that produce for the consumer market. The following list highlights some of the most important new consumer characteristics and attitudes that companies need to take into consideration today:

- Erosion of trust in business and government
- Perceived loss of privacy
- Concern about personal data collection by business and government
- Increased concern about personal and family finances

- Increased concern about the national economy
- Concern about the implications of global warming
- Increased interest in aging and wellness issues of active baby boomers
- Increased life expectancy and senior populations
- Growing impact of teen and preteen consumers
- Increase in ethnic and racial population diversity
- Greater product and pricing sophistication through Internet use

These changes have significantly expanded the number of focus groups that market researchers must monitor and that marketers must target.

The changes imply changes in marketing approach. For example, a perceived loss of privacy has made consumers resent accustomed telemarketing approaches that interrupt their private lives with phone calls and product pushes. Likewise, a lack of trust in business and government suggests that product approvals and recommendations from commercial or government agencies may not carry the same weight with consumers as they have in earlier years. At the same time, baby boomers may be increasingly approachable through advertising and promotion ties that involve planning for the future; thus, selling time-shares in Florida should perhaps emphasize the investment value of the purchase along with the long-term pleasure of the location and climate.

We need no hypothetical examples to understand how marketing has risen to take advantage of the increasing power of the teen and preteen markets. We see the results everywhere, and they are growing steadily, in the forms of new chains of clothing stores; massive teen- and preteen-oriented marketing campaigns for electronic gadgets and entertainment in music, film, television, magazines, and games; and advertising and features on the Internet.

Approaches to an increasingly diverse population are sweeping many other markets as well. Advertising and promotion now feature models of all races and ethnic backgrounds, and many more different ages and body builds appear. People with gray hair, people with disabilities, and even people wearing glasses used to be omitted from the ads—but they appear frequently now as marketers come to appreciate the growing buying power of people of all different kinds.

"Money talks," and nowhere is it talking as fast or as much as through the astonishing and interactive appeal and global reach of the Internet. Technology is creating many novel possibilities for marketing researchers. The Internet provides the opportunity for accessing timely information and having real-time dialogues with millions of consumers, at a small fraction of the cost of direct mail or traditional media advertising.

Rapid transportation and high-speed communication bring quick access to products and services as well as information. Globalization creates both the opportunity and the need for research that analyzes differences in cultures, tastes, and business practices. Growing competition from other countries such as Argentina, Australia, Brazil, Chile, China and Taiwan, India, Japan, Korea, Mexico, New Zealand, Russia, Vietnam, and many more has brought a new urgency to the need for increasingly effective marketing research and practices.

In order to grow, companies must use their resources to increase the sales of existing products or introduce new ones. One of the most important decisions facing marketing managers is whether to develop new products.

Successful new products can generate huge profits for a company, while products that fail can be a company's undoing. Because of the cost of developing and launching a new product in today's highly competitive market, most companies cannot afford failures—but they do occur, nonetheless.

Sometimes products that we have enjoyed and used for an extended time will suddenly disappear from the shelves. Good products that are ineffectively marketed can be as unprofitable as inferior products that should never have been produced. While success depends on the entire marketing process working as it should, it all begins with marketing research. If a company has lost track of the true preferences of its consumer base or is not marketing effectively enough to the consumer base that wants its products, it may find itself rapidly losing market share.

The tide always seems to run out faster than it comes in, and if a company sees its profit margin shrinking, then your favorite cereal—or suntan lotion, shirts, shoes, eye shadow, and even cars and motor homes—may be taken off the consumer market forever. Immediately, these products are replaced by new products that have also been intensely researched and that are perceived by the financial and administrative managers of their companies as having a better chance of successful competition in the ever-changing marketplace.

THE MARKETING RESEARCH PROCESS

"Selling the sizzle" and "keeping your finger on the pulse of the buyer" are old slogans of advertising and marketing that date back to the 1920s and 1930s. They say something about the intense interest in people's preferences and the bracing climate of constant change that have always characterized this field.

Discovering What the Consumer Really Wants

"Sell the sizzle" was a reminder to employees in the marketing, promotion, and advertising industry that people didn't buy a steak just because it was a high-protein food. The "sell" was supposed to give people a sensory reminder of something they wanted: a steak because it smelled and tasted terrific. The best marketing approach reminded potential buyers of the sound of that steak sizzling as it cooked, the aromas engulfing them as they imagined how good it was going to taste. "Selling the sizzle" was the strategy that would make the customer *want* to buy the steak.

To do an effective job of marketing, it is essential to understand your consumers' likes and dislikes. You have to find out what it is that they really want. The men and women of the marketing industry of the 1920s and 1930s had to fly pretty much by the seat of their pants. A good hunch would be followed up by discussion with colleagues and by study of the meager existing data on population and of other products the people had been buying for a long time. Door-to-door surveys were sometimes used in specific neighborhoods and small towns, as were street-corner surveys in larger cities. By the 1940s through the 1970s, telephone surveys became much more prevalent, and survey forms were also sometimes sent out by mail to carefully structured lists of potential responders. Listing services specialized in maintaining databases of names, addresses, and phone numbers for these surveys and for use in advertising for mail-order sales. One Madison Avenue listing service owner remarked that, in 1960, a 7 percent response to a direct mailing campaign was a very respectable success. Today, highly targeted direct-mail campaigns claim response rates between 0.5 percent and 10 percent, but the average response rate reported in a Direct Marketing Association study in 2005 was 2.61 percent.

If those earlier market researchers could see the vastly increased power that technology has put into the hands of marketers today, they would be astonished. They would push their broad-brimmed hats back from their foreheads, hang up their black dial telephones, and whistle an admiring "Whew!" upon observing how readily marketing professionals today can access demographics on millions—and billions—of potential customers. Surveys, direct-mail campaigns, and interactive campaigns for electronic media can be tailored to very specific target audiences, and returns for the best-focused may run to 40 percent, 60 percent, or even better. The size of today's financial risks would probably flabbergast yesterday's professionals, too. Back then, hardly anyone was talking about multimillion-dollar initial product offerings or multinational markets. Today we are talking about consumer markets numbering in the billions. And it is that change that has made market research increasingly important in all the ensuing years.

Early companies that have survived and that have had a major impact on the marketing research field today include A. C. Nielsen and Harris International. The Nielsen Ratings and the Harris Polls are two of the most famous and influential of the long-standing marketing research mechanisms in the world. Other notable organizations of this type include Strategic Intelligence Group and MarketProbe. By visiting their websites, you can get an overview of the broad range of services offered by major marketing research firms today.

As the world's population has grown, the markets have grown—in complexity as well as potential. It continues to be true, however, that if you are going to invest a lot of money and risk it in producing and selling a product, you had better know who your customers are, what they like and will buy, and even—with the best educated guess that money can buy—what they are going to like and will buy in the future. That's the market researcher's job.

Today, in multinational markets, with competition for many products streaming live and crisscrossing the globe into every local market from all over the world, it is not always possible to know personally just why your potential customers are going to want to "buy the steak." "Selling the sizzle" won't get your product any market share at all if the broadest part of your best new-consumer base happens to be vegetarian. In a more diverse, multicultural, and/or multinational marketplace, we need to know a lot more, and we need to know it more quickly, because the nature of our customer bases is changing and shifting with increasing speed as our world changes.

Keeping a Finger on the Pulse of the Buyer

Rapid growth and change make it necessary to continually move quickly and systematically to keep up with market demand. Powerful, state-of-the-art technology and refined marketing analysis techniques provide the accurate and timely information that is integral to the marketing research process. The modern systems approach to marketing information is greatly facilitated by advances in computer technology that enable orderly collection, analysis, and dissemination of the information to key decision makers.

In large companies, managers specify the kind, amount, and quality of information that they require and turn these specifications over to their marketing research departments.

Marketing research is a process that uses specific steps or systems to arrive at its goals, and they usually occur more or less in the following sequence:

1. Identifying and defining an opportunity, such as a target or "niche" market or an unfilled need
2. Collecting and analyzing the data relevant to this opportunity, including the size and nature of the potential market, the size and nature of the competition, reasons why a new product can succeed, projections of quantities of the product that can be sold and at what price the consumers will be able and willing to buy it, and the nature of the changes in the market that can be expected in the future
3. Presenting the information first to the marketing manager and then to other corporate managers, such as those for corporate development, product planning and design, finance, production or manufacturing, advertising and promotion, sales, and customer service

Although some new-product ideas originate with market research, an idea can come from any source, including from the company's competitors.

In the automobile industry, for example, Japan illustrated the adage that imitation is the sincerest form of flattery by improving on already developed American automobile products and then capturing the largest share of the American market. In general, it succeeded with smaller, less expensive cars that got better gas mileage, lasted longer, and required fewer repairs less often.

Subsequently, in the face of the overwhelming success of that competition and its damaging effects, the American car manufacturers underwent a series of transformations, modifying their own products to be smaller and achieve more fuel economy—and also manufacturing some of their parts in other countries, at a much lower labor cost. Many American workers were laid off, and the American public began to exhibit some animosity toward Japanese-made cars.

With that change in the market, the Japanese manufacturers moved some of their manufacturing to the United States, as well. This industry continues to be characterized by extreme competition and upheaval, and this reality is felt especially in the United States in its effects on the steel industry and the labor market. It is also an industry in which we can expect deep market changes in the near future as the manufacturers confront the major challenges of global warming and global oil shortages.

Market researchers in the automobile industry are under pressure to provide adequate information and analyses to corporate managers who face massive changes in manufacturing processes as well as in the types and capacities of the products they will produce in the future.

Today, intense competition in other industries has evolved from several countries of Asia. China, India, Japan, Singapore, South Korea, and others have moved to the forefront of world commerce through sophisticated technology and market research. Their marketing researchers collect information on every aspect of American culture and technology to plan highly effective and competitive sales campaigns, not only for automobiles and trucks but also for investment and financial products, electronics, entertainment, publishing, toys, biotechnology, food products, clothing, pet supplies, housewares, industrial and military machinery and tools, and myriad other products.

Euro-market companies have also moved ahead in many areas, such as electronics, biotechnology, photonics, and medical and scientific products. Russia and other former Soviet Union countries have begun to compete significantly in global markets as well. Likewise, many of the Arab nations and South Africa are now well represented in U.S. and U.K. financial and real estate markets, among others. Wars, poverty, and extreme climatic problems have held back much of the Middle East and Africa, but with recent advances in technology and global communications, some countries in those areas are gaining more strength in diversified commercial fields and will soon become more commercially powerful, global players in their own right.

American, Canadian, and United Kingdom marketing research departments must have a clear understanding of worldwide competition's approach to the consumers of international markets, as well as an understanding of their companies' customers and potential customers, both now and for the future. Analysts must carefully monitor changing needs, purchasing capacities, lifestyles, and tastes in order to predict what people will want in the future.

Global demographics have produced some unexpected insights into international markets. In the American markets, a burgeoning teen population is influencing both new products and the manner in which they are marketed. This trend is of increasing importance in other markets as well. The most global market of all comprises urban and suburban teens around the world, who exhibit similar tastes and attitudes. An affectation of often disdainful attitudes, establishment-defying fashion and grooming combinations, and passion for the newest technologies characterize a substantial, if not totally representative, international teen market that is being exploited today by numerous global industries, such as electronics, music and entertainment, fashion, and makeup and grooming products.

Teens are only one of many special consumer groups being served by new and focused marketing. Other larger groups in the United States include African Americans, Hispanics/Latinos, women, and seniors. Marketers have targeted these groups in the past, but today's economy has further diversified them into dozens of specific subgroups defined by age, lifestyle, neighborhood, and combinations of these and other characteristics that affect their buying habits. It is up to marketing researchers to learn about these numerous market segments and define their future buying trends.

Developing New Products. Many of the ideas for new products come from trends identified through marketing research. Depending on the product, development can take a long time. For example, years of development and testing are required from the time an automobile design leaves the drawing board until the finished product hits the showroom floor. As a consequence, many products are rendered obsolete during the development cycle by the introduction of competitors' products or technological innovations.

WORK OF MARKETING RESEARCHERS

Marketing research professionals engage daily in numerous research activities, including the ones in the following list:

Developing customer profiles
Researching characteristics of potential new consumers
Monitoring competitors
Identifying market trends
Testing new products and evaluating consumer response
Analyzing brand images
Assisting with advertising and promotion campaigns
Evaluating the success of advertising and promotions

These research activities involve a variety of methods for collecting and analyzing data from multiple sources.

Acquiring and Using Primary Data

Primary data is collected through original research for a specific purpose, and this process is usually costly. Primary data can come from other company personnel, actual and potential customers, analysis of competitors, and other sources. This data is normally obtained through observation, experimentation, surveying, and electronic data collection.

1. **Observation.** Consumer purchasing behavior can be observed and recorded in stores, parking lots, and other places where people commonly gather to buy or use goods. For instance, by direct observation on-site, a market researcher for a toy company can learn which displays in a toy department attract children's attention and which ones attract parents' attention. Similarly, observation of a sports arena parking lot can tell a market researcher what percentage of sports patrons in that area drive

passenger cars, SUVs, campers, or vans. In a simple example of customer observation, the marketing department of a major daily newspaper wanted to increase its market share of horse-racing customers. It sent a small team of market researchers armed with handheld counters out to the track. As customers entered the grounds and walked along toward the grandstand, the researchers could readily observe various newspapers and the "Daily Racing Form" sticking out of people's pockets, rolled up under their arms, and actually being read. The researchers tallied the various papers and, at day's end, had a good idea of which publications' racing sections were preferred.

2. **Experimentation**. Market research by experimentation means trying out a new-product, marketing, pricing, or packaging idea. In the food industry, it may include taste tests. In the retail food industry, it may include trying out and comparing the effectiveness of island displays versus shelf displays, or of shelf displays and cross-marketing (putting food products with other related items—foods for summer barbecues with barbecue equipment, for example). Experimentation may include measuring the effects of advertising, price changes, or product or packaging alterations on consumer buying practices.

3. **Surveying.** Researchers conduct surveys by mail, telephone, or the Internet, as well as in person, to get consumer reactions to existing or proposed products. The survey may be designed in-house and may also be conducted by staff members, or it may be outsourced. If outsourcing is elected, the in-house market researcher will oversee having it done by a survey company that specializes in planning, designing, writing, and carrying out market research surveys—by telephone, direct mail, customer contact (as in supermarkets or other high-traffic areas), the Internet, or other media. Listing services may be used to provide specifically targeted lists of consumers' names, addresses, phone numbers, ages, product preferences, buying patterns, or other types of data that will help to make the surveys successful.

4. **Electronic Data Collection.** This method uses databank information gathered by various retail chain stores and by financial and market research groups, nationally and internationally. Some organizations, such as major supermarkets and discount stores, do their own data collection, monitoring their consumers' behavior by purchase amounts, product types, and even time of month or time of day. These forms of primary (and proprietary) data can help them to decide whether to purchase more of certain

items nearer to paydays at the end of the month, or whether to increase or decrease their stock of certain items in general.

Organizations that do not collect data on their own can purchase secondary information from marketing research organizations for their marketing purposes. Some of these research organizations are so large that their data acquisitions cover consumers in entire countries and beyond, but thanks to computerized analysis, they are able to supply their clients with specific data even for the smallest targeted groups of consumers.

Acquiring and Using Secondary Data

Secondary data comprises information that has been previously collected inside or outside the firm and may be part of company records or large databases. Since this type of information is usually cheaper and faster to acquire than primary data, researchers normally begin the research process by collecting and analyzing all relevant secondary data.

Sources of secondary data include information that is available from international organizations such as the United Nations, the World Health Organization, the World Bank, various NGOs (nongovernmental organizations), and others that maintain economic, demographic, and related records. The United States and other national governments also provide many kinds of useful data, including census figures, labor and economic statistics, and detailed demographic records. Additional sources include industry and professional associations, state and local governments, unions, local public and private libraries, publishers, commercial databases, and special-interest groups. Many of these can be accessed through the Internet, as can many other new sources, both within the United States and internationally.

Marketing researchers provide their organizations' managers with the data, analyses, conclusions, and recommendations needed to develop an informed marketing strategy, including potential market share, sales figures, prices, promotions, and channels of distribution.

Market Research Roles in Product Development

When companies decide to consider the development of new products, designers create prototypes—or trial models—on the basis of market research. The prototypes are then tested for marketability. Marketing research professionals may oversee the market testing, compile the results, and make recommendations, in more or less elaborate reports that are delivered to management on paper or in multimedia presentations, as needed. Management's options may then include abandoning development, altering the product in some way and continuing the research, or planning the promotion strategy. Marketing researchers are part of product development teams and contribute needed information to the entire product development process. Marketing's role in product development is discussed in more detail in Chapter 3.

The scope of marketing research is not limited to the marketability of consumer products. Research may be conducted regarding environmental concerns, business decisions, political campaigns, association images, and a range of other areas.

Regardless of the particular research question or problem, all research involves data collection and analysis. It may be quantitative in nature, involving numerical data, or qualitative, dealing with subjective information such as opinions and attitudes. Thus, individuals pursuing marketing research as a career should have strong backgrounds in computer science, mathematics and statistics, psychology, and communications.

Marketing research techniques in the past relied primarily on the measurement of verbal communication via such instruments as surveys, focus groups, and questionnaires. One problem with the use of surveys and questionnaires is that consumers' responses regarding quantities of a particular item that they think they will buy often vary quite a bit from the actual quantities that they do eventually buy. Frequently, nonverbal images can be used instead to elicit consumers' thoughts and feelings most effectively. A relatively new method, called ZMET, uses pictures rather than words to gain insights into how consumers think and behave. Such companies as AT&T Corporation, Coca-Cola Company, DuPont, Eastman Kodak Company, General Motors Corporation, Lifetime Entertainment Services, Pacific Gas & Electric, Polaroid Corporation, and Reebok International have used ZMET in various ways to learn customer attitudes about brands, products, companies, product concepts and designs, product usage and purchase experiences, life experiences, and/or habitual consumption patterns.

MARKETING RESEARCH ONLINE

Computer technology is having a profound effect on the field of marketing research. Powerful computers enable marketers to compile extensive databases in-house to analyze their customers, and Internet-based marketing research offers still more improved access to information. External information is available through highly specialized marketing research agencies whose services can be directly accessed via the Internet.

Access to online information has opened many more sources of information to researchers and, to some extent, has changed the nature of marketing research. Mass marketing of the 1950s and '60s usually presented the same message and product to all consumers. This approach was then refined into market segments that divided consumers into smaller groups with common characteristics.

Today's database marketing enables marketers to target enormous populations and identify specific consumer segments in precise detail, all the way down to the level of the individual consumer. Data on individual buying practices and preferences are acquired from bank and credit card use, purchases through discount clubs and the Internet, warranty cards, sweepstakes, forms that buyers complete when making purchases, and many other methods. All of this information is electronically harvested and entered into massive databases. Powerful software extracts common characteristics of users of specific products. This information is then analyzed and incorporated into the development of new products, advertising strategies, and every aspect of the marketing process. These national and international databases are continually updated, and such database-marketing programs have now become "business as usual."

POSITIONS IN MARKETING RESEARCH

Marketing researchers must perform data-intensive work, but they must also use logic in their field. Hiring and advancement depends on how effective they are in both areas. According to recruiters, the best jobs are going to applicants who are especially adept in analyzing and reaching narrow market subgroups with greater purchasing power, extreme brand loyalty, or other prime characteristics.

Manufacturers of goods or services may either staff internal marketing research departments or hire outside firms to perform the function. The keener the competition, the more important the role that marketing research plays. This role is further determined by the size of the organization and its need for research.

Director of Marketing Research. In companies with marketing research departments, the director of marketing research usually reports to the marketing manager, who coordinates information from marketing research with technical research and product development input. The director of marketing research works with the marketing manager in specifying research projects. These projects are then assigned to analysts, who work with other members of the marketing research department in a team effort. The director decides when outside specialists are needed, contracts with them, and coordinates their activities with those of the internal personnel throughout the research process.

Though a standard career path might be from analyst to senior analyst to assistant manager to manager, in the more organic organizations of today a new analyst might be introduced into a team with a project already in progress or may be given a list of ongoing projects and be expected to contribute to their progress.

Junior Marketing Research Analyst. New graduates are hired usually as junior or associate analysts. Entry-level jobs may involve such mundane work as handling correspondence and proofreading questionnaires, but during the first year, the junior analyst will also be involved in developing surveys, analyzing data, organizing studies, and writing reports.

As in every job, the activities assigned to the entry-level worker depend on the worker's ability to execute the tasks and the projects currently under way in the department. Understanding that the first year is, at least to some extent, a training year, the new worker should view this opportunity as a practical learning experience and should be prepared to assume whatever duties are assigned.

Field Service Director. The field service director hires field service personnel, including interviewers and coders, to perform specialized tasks and directs their efforts. Workers in field services conduct interviews by phone or in person, asking questions that have been written by research analysts in charge of a project. Coders or tabulation personnel enter numbers into the computer and run standard types of programs. These programs produce the initial reports that provide the basis for further analysis.

Field service and tabulations personnel usually do not need college degrees, often work for relatively low wages, and do not normally advance to other positions in marketing research. College students sometimes work part-time as interviewers or coders to gain experience in that aspect of marketing research.

The field service director, on the other hand, is an integral part of the organization's marketing research process. The director may have begun as a junior analyst and been promoted. Depending on skills and performance, the field service director may be promoted to analyst or senior analyst positions. In smaller companies, junior analysts are likely to be involved in interviewing and coding.

Sometimes field and tabulation work is contracted out to field service firms. The director of field services oversees any arrangements, contracts, and communications with these firms, establishes initial guidelines and any specific training that might be required, and monitors the performance of the contract workers.

Marketing Research Analyst. Once junior analysts demonstrate an understanding of the research process and the ability to analyze data and relate conclusions to the specifics of the project, the next logical step is promotion to the position of analyst. A marketing research analyst works with managers to gather background material and develop proposals for research projects. Analysts with two or three years of experience work fairly independently on their own projects.

Communicating tactfully and courteously with managers regarding pet projects is germane to career success. Sometimes research reveals that certain projects are not viable. The analyst must present these results as thoroughly and professionally as possible. Although number crunching is an important part of marketing research, human relations skills are equally important.

Senior Marketing Research Analyst. With sufficient solid experience, usually after four or five years, successful analysts may be promoted to senior analyst or marketing research manager. Senior analysts may spearhead research projects or function as advisers for other analysts. Although one senior analyst is responsible for each project, the analyst may confer with other senior analysts as needed for suggestions or solutions to problems that arise during the project.

Marketing research requires teamwork. The senior analyst supervises the work of junior analysts, coordinates the input of everyone involved in the project, and presents the conclusions. The senior analyst works with, and sometimes under, a research manager. This manager serves in a consulting capacity and, if employed by a marketing research firm, may well have been the individual instrumental in getting the client's business. A central part of the senior analyst's job in marketing research firms is obtaining new accounts and maintaining contacts with clients.

Marketing Research Director. The director of the marketing research department in a company or other organization holds the department's top position and assumes its requisite responsibilities and headaches. The person serving in the capacity of director is the liaison between the department and the rest of the company. Staffing the department, preparing the budget, overseeing all projects, and reporting to the marketing manager periodically are all part of the job. In marketing research firms, the top position—president of the firm—is usually held by the owner or a partner. In this role, bringing in new business is a big part of the job. The head of a firm is also concerned with satisfying the demands of clients rather than upper-level management. Still, whether marketing research is done in a department or by a marketing research firm, the activities performed by analysts are basically the same.

Regardless of the position held, marketing research professionals work under a certain amount of pressure. An analyst may work on more than one project at a time and face multiple deadlines. Because analysts are assigned total responsibility for projects, the buck stops with them. They are highly accountable for success or failure even though, as in all research, some variables are beyond their control. As an analyst, one is subject to the priorities of others. For example, the marketing manager may dictate the analyst's schedule, requiring the analyst to stop work on one project at a crucial time and take on something else deemed more urgent by upper management. Nonetheless, the work is both challenging and rewarding.

Marketing researchers are the pioneers of marketing—exploring new possibilities that sometimes result in revolutionary new products that may make the lives of many people easier, healthier, or more enjoyable.

OPPORTUNITIES IN MARKETING RESEARCH

Executives in marketing research struggle to find talented new people to fill numerous positions. Not only do today's researchers need statistical knowledge, but they must also be skilled in the use of databases, current software, and the Internet. Over the last couple of decades, many universities have been attempting to increase their numbers of marketing research students.

In 2006, about 260,000 market and survey researchers were employed in the United States, with around 234,000 being market research analysts, and the rest survey researchers. *The Occupational Outlook Handbook* of the Bureau of Labor Statistics has projected somewhat faster-than-average growth for market researchers in the United States between 2006 and 2016.

The *ESOMAR Directory of Research Organizations* lists more than 1,800 major research organizations worldwide as of 2005, and this number is expected to increase rapidly in the decade between 2006 and 2016. ESOMAR, the powerful, sixty-year-old, European Society for Opinion and Marketing Research, has led the industry with its code of ethics and its high standards. ESOMAR's mission statement says that it is "the world organization for enabling better research into markets, consumers, and societies." Headquartered in the Netherlands, ESOMAR is "resolutely nonpolitical" and has approximately 4,500 members, representing more than a hundred countries. The organization publishes *Research World* magazine as well as other publications that provide a wealth of information about the public relations industry and its career possibilities worldwide.

Growth in the field of marketing research is a testimonial to its effectiveness. All kinds and sizes of businesses are engaged in marketing research. Nonprofit hospitals use marketing research to project growth, while for-profit hospitals employ it in marketing; colleges use it to target potential students and allocate resources among academic areas; and nonprofit organizations look to marketing research to determine who contributes and how best to solicit donations.

While large manufacturers of consumer goods staff marketing research departments, major growth in the field is occurring in the increasing numbers of independent research firms and Internet companies. Some of these firms employ forty or more people, but most are small and often specialize—for example, in educational institutions, hospitals, nonprofit organizations, or a particular type of consumer good or service.

Expanding service industries such as financial and business services, cable television, health, and leisure activities also use marketing research firms. Some major retail tracking firms supply information on how well various products are selling and where. Outstanding examples are A. C. Nielsen Company, which pioneered retail tracking in the 1920s, and Information Resources, which is a relative newcomer to the field.

It is wise for anyone interested in marketing research to develop career objectives with some area of specialization in mind.

Advances in information technology combined with the commitment from top management to have up-to-date and accurate information have contributed to the growth in marketing research. Today, data analysis can be done in a small fraction of the time that was required in the past because of more powerful computer hardware and software. Sophisticated multivariate statistical analyses yield information that would be too cumbersome to derive using manual means. This type of analysis takes some of the guesswork out of producing and marketing new products. As both domestic and foreign competition place more pressure on companies to produce successful products, managers will rely more and more on marketing research information to make their decisions.

At least an undergraduate degree is required for entry into marketing research. This degree may be in any of a number of areas, including statistics, psychology, computer science, marketing, or another business major. The particular major is less important than skills in math, statistics, computers, research design and analysis, and both written and oral communications.

As mentioned previously, a career objective that focuses on a specific industry in which the applicant has knowledge or experience is helpful. The best chance for a beginner to break into the field is to gain relevant experience as a student, such as through part-time or summer jobs doing interviewing or data entry, involvement in research projects, directed independent study to hone research skills, or an internship in a marketing research department or firm.

Salaries for marketing research professionals vary considerably according to the size of the firm, level of responsibility, geographical location, and other factors that are discussed in more detail in Chapter 11. The *Occupational Outlook Handbook* reported median annual earnings of market research analysts in mid-2006 as $58,000, with the lowest 10 percent making less than $32,250 and the highest 10 percent making more than $112,250. Most of these workers were employed in the computer systems/design/services industry; management of companies and enterprises; and other technical, professional, scientific, management, and consulting services.

Median annual earnings of the survey research group in mid-2006 were reported as $33,360, with the lowest 10 percent earning less than $16,720 and the highest 10 percent earning more than $73,630.

This wage data was derived by the U.S. Department of Labor from the Occupational Employment Statistics (OES) survey program.

ADDITIONAL SOURCES OF INFORMATION

Key professional publications such as *Marketing News* can provide familiarity with marketing research terms and give a good overview of the industry. *Honomichi Global*, published by Inside Research, issues a selected list of the "twenty-five best" marketing research firms.

Trade associations are an excellent source for up-to-date career information. Information may also be obtained from the following marketing research organizations:

Association for Consumer Research
Labovitz School of Business and Economics
University of Minnesota Duluth
11 E. Superior St., Ste. 210
Duluth, MN 55802
acrwebsite.org
Publishes the *Journal for Consumer Research*.

Council of American Survey Research Organizations
170 N. Country Rd., Ste. 4
Port Jefferson, NY 11777
casro.org

ESOMAR International Research Organization
Vondelstraat 172
1054 GV Amsterdam
The Netherlands
Publishes *Research World* magazine and *ESOMAR International Code of Marketing and Social Research Practice.*

Kellogg School of Management
Department of Marketing Research
Northwestern University
Evanston, IL 60201
kelloggschool.edu

Marketing Research Association
110 National Dr.
Glastonbury, CT 06033
mra-net.org

World Advertising Research Center
Farm Road, Henley on Thames
Oxfordshire RG9 1EJ
United Kingdom
Publishes *Admap* magazine.

CHAPTER 3

CAREERS IN PRODUCT DEVELOPMENT

The term *product* refers to all of the things that are made to serve a particular use. Products include both goods and services. Bees produce both goods and services, in making honey and caring for their young and their queen. The human community also produces goods and services: goods such as computers and books, and services such as nursing care and consulting.

Some goods and services are produced for direct consumption, and others are produced to be sold and traded. The latter are called commercial products.

In the third quarter of 2007, the market (or commercial) value of the United States' output of goods and services (referred to as the gross domestic product, or GDP) was valued by the U.S. Department of Commerce's Bureau of Economic Analysis (BEA) at $13,970,500,000,000, or $13,970.5 billion. Statistics for the output of individual industries and particular regions of the country can be obtained on the Web at bea.gov.

Most goods and services are developed only after careful and extensive research, analysis, and planning. In most modern corporations, this process is carried out by the product developers, who are the company employees charged with managing the development of commercial products—whether they are goods or services—so that they will serve consumers' needs, sell reliably well, and be respectably profitable for the organization that has produced them.

Most large corporations manage this function within a research and development, or R&D, department. In the late 1960s, the U.S. government began to give fewer tax incentives to corporations for their R&D. One law made it impossible for corporations to deduct R&D expenses from their taxes unless the expenses were against income earned by the product in the same fiscal year. This approach to taxation made it difficult for companies involved in long-term research—anything over one year—to develop their products. Some historians have blamed this trend for certain advantages gained by other countries over the United States in various industries.

R&D is essential for the development of successful new products, and many companies and professional and trade associations continue to work hard to regain and protect tax and other incentives that support solid, in-depth research and development.

THE IMPORTANCE OF PRODUCT DEVELOPMENT

In early times, products prepared for trade were simple and few. Some examples were tools made of sharpened stones and bones, cleaned furs and animal skins, and polished shells. Product development and manufacture could easily be handled by just one person.

A little later came woven cloth and baskets, clay pots and bowls, metal weapons and jewelry, and eventually carvings, spices, perfumes, and trade in exotic items from faraway lands. Still, product development was relatively straightforward. A ship's captain or other trader might simply estimate how many carved wooden chests he could trade or sell back home and how closely he would have to watch over the production in the foreign land where he was getting them, and his product development was complete.

In modern times, product development is a whole different animal, in both the developed and developing nations of the world.

The "Most Wanted Products" cited by CNET.com for one week of the winter of 2007–2008 included the following:

- Nintendo Wii
- Epson Stylus Photo R1900
- Sony PlayStation 3 (60GB)
- Logitech diNovo Mini Keyboard
- LG Voyager VX (Verizon Wireless)

These products make up a revealing lineup of electronic devices. CNET .com provides an updated "Most Wanted Products" listing each week, covering cell phones, desktops, digital cameras, laptops, MP3 players, televisions, and many other categories. Each of these products is the result of complex and extended research and development. CNET's list dynamically illustrates the tremendous power of the product development process that takes place in our modern global marketplace.

Modern electronic products such as these embody intricate, complex designs and can cost a fortune to make. Raw materials and manufactured components may have to be brought together from several countries. The needs, wants, and tastes of consumers in a wide variety of cultures may have to be met. Costs may be affected by frequently changing embargoes, customs and duties, taxes, and transportation costs, as well as the direct costs of original materials and labor. The product developer must be aware of a broad range of information and be able to plan to minimize the costs and maximize all of the opportunities that exist.

COMPLEX PRODUCTION AND MULTIFACETED GLOBAL MARKETS

Global markets today are characterized by vast numbers of competing producers of goods and services, rapid daily exchange of raw materials and of partially processed and fully completed goods, quickly fluctuating investments, and detailed communication from all parts of the world. Mass production by machines, applications of electric power, and enormous population growth, along with other forces, have contributed to a production world that turns out millions of objects to be sold in a mind-boggling variety of global markets. Production on this scale represents an enormous investment of time, money, and material and requires highly skilled and accurate product planning and development.

No one can ever be 100 percent perfect in planning and developing profitable products, but product developers are some of the specialists who, nevertheless, have the responsibility for making workable, profitable, and predictably successful products. Certainly some fields are less complex than others, but in all fields, the work of the product developer today is fast-changing, challenging, and complex. It can also be exciting and satisfying.

Every year, an endless number of fascinating new products make their entrance to the market. Multifuel automobiles, electronic games and handheld wonder gadgets, smart maps, home health monitors, antiaging products, next-generation televisions, faster and more powerful personalized computers, and thousands of other products are the brainstorms of product development professionals.

Marketing begins with observing, perceiving, and understanding the needs and desires of the market. Products are usually conceived with particular markets in mind. For example, companies are continually introducing a host of new products to capture the four- to twelve-year-old market. Electronic toys, games, clothes, books, DVDs, movies, television shows, greeting cards, and all sorts of new products designed to appeal to that age-group will continue to flow into this steadily expanding market.

THE ELECTRONIC GOODS AND SERVICES REVOLUTION

In the United States and in almost all developed and developing countries alike, the market for electronic goods and services to all age-groups continues to expand as more people feel the need to buy advanced cell phones, televisions, computers, software, communication devices, and entertainment players of all kinds. Toys, communication and entertainment games and devices, such as iPods, MP3 players, BlackBerries, and Game Boys, have captured the imaginations and desires of billions of consumers worldwide.

Most of this desire has been created by intelligent marketing, in surveying, understanding, and exploiting the needs and desires of people in different cultures all over the globe. The expansion of these markets has continued almost uninterrupted for more than three decades. In all this time, economic recessions, floods and droughts, civil wars and invasions, and other significant factors that have slowed regional economies have failed to slow the overall pace of the electronic products revolution.

NEW KINDS OF ECONOMIC NEEDS

Today, however, major economic changes are being brought about by the surging costs of wars, the damage wrought to human living areas and crops by severe weather changes and natural disasters, and the overriding implications of global warming. The scope of these changes is forcing new attitudes toward the nature of economic growth that profoundly affect the product planning and development processes. New concern is arising about the proliferation of disposable items, outsized packaging, and the many other wasteful policies that continue to contribute significantly to the destruction of Earth's atmospheric protections.

It is the job of marketing researchers to gather and analyze these fluctuating market conditions and inform the product developers of their implications. Product developers must then propose new and modified products and marketing strategies that are appropriate to the consumers' changing needs and desires. Perhaps future products should be lower in cost, more durable, more portable, and more easily expanded rather than discarded.

Many marketing industry commentators suggested in 2006 that companies should expect to produce more kinds of products, specifically target products to many more smaller markets, and meet demand for less expensive, more economical, longer-lasting, and more environmentally friendly products. The American automobile market, for one, has begun to focus on environmentally friendly cars, and competition for fuel efficiency in automobile products is gaining rapid momentum. Many European and Asian industries have also begun to produce more consumer goods to meet these needs.

PDMA AWARDS FOR INNOVATIVE PRODUCT DEVELOPMENT

Established companies must continually develop products to compete with new innovative products that appear on the market. In 2007, the PDMA (Product Development and Management Association) gave its Outstanding Corporate Innovator Award to two organizations: Mine Safety Appliance Company (MSA) and FedEx Corporation.

MSA was cited for its "disciplined new product development (NPD) process that transformed a 96-year-old company into a global leader in sophisticated safety products." In 1996, the company began a process to discover best practices worldwide and to integrate the discoveries into its internal processes and new-product development planning. MSA has applied both traditional and emerging technologies to create innovative product offerings that now represent more than 30 percent of the company's revenue.

The achievement of FedEx Corporation in developing new products and services on a continuing basis, as a "true industry pioneer," was also cited. In 2000, FedEx launched a company-wide campaign for transforming its new-product management practices. It focused on new strategic market segmentation and utilized global expansion and acquisitions to form the foundation for applying new processes and concepts. The result has been new service offerings that have extended and reinforced the company's leadership position in packaging and shipping.

The Product Development and Management Association is a professional association with more than three thousand members worldwide. It fosters support for professionals in the field and supplies information and resources for education, networking, collaboration, certification, and recognition. Its publications include the *Journal of Product Innovation Management* and *Visions* magazine, and it sponsors seminars and conferences in various locations throughout the year. For more information, go to pdma.org.

DRIVERS OF NEW-PRODUCT DEVELOPMENT

The constant demand for new products drives product development efforts. Companies try to give consumers what they want, when and where they want it, at a price they are willing to pay. This involves management decisions pertaining to the marketing mix, otherwise known as the "four *P*s:"

- Product
- Place
- Promotion
- Price

Marketing managers assemble product development teams to help make these essential decisions and shepherd a product through the development process. Whether companies can survive and profit in the competitive marketplace depends on the effectiveness of these teams.

PRODUCT DEVELOPMENT DIMENSIONS AND PROCESS

New-product development today has three dimensions:

- New customer applications
- New customer groups
- Alternative technologies

The sports sandal company Teva, a global leader in the high-performance sports sandals market, was founded by a young Colorado River guide who realized a need. He wanted a high-quality sandal that would stay on his feet during rough-and-tumble activity and in sometimes fast-moving water.

The sandal had to be strong enough to provide protection from sharp stones, nonskid for safety, and light and flexible enough not to inhibit movement. It also had to fit the foot perfectly. He tried different materials and approaches to the shape and line until he was satisfied. The sandal he created was a masterpiece of elegance and durability. At first, he and a few friends were the only people wearing his sandals, but the reputation spread, and demand grew. This innovative outdoorsman has received multiple U.S. patents for his unique designs, and his technological innovations help Teva products lead the market.

Innovation is not just a one-shot phenomenon. One of the most prolific companies in the field of new-product development is Rubbermaid. This manufacturer of more than five thousand different products introduces new products at a rate of roughly one per day, with nine out of ten becoming successes. This astonishing percentage does not even include the products that are improved versions of other products! Who generates all of these ideas for products? As many as twenty teams comprising several people each from a variety of departments, such as marketing, manufacturing, research and development, and finance, cooperate in the process. Even top management does its share. Once, two top executives touring the British Museum's Egyptian exhibits returned to the United States with eleven ideas for new products. Along with a variety of kitchen and bath utensils, mailboxes, storage containers, cleaning aids, and tackle boxes, Rubbermaid offers a line of products for the youth market, including toys, makeup organizers, lunch boxes, and drink bottles.

New products benefit from association, and brand recognition builds with the continuity of one successful product after another. Product development sometimes involves developing an entire line of products. Black & Decker took notice of the rapid expansion of the Home Depot chain of stores and the popular television show "Home Improvement" and generated billions of dollars in home improvement products, to become a top-ranked company in the field.

Even extremely successful companies are confronted with developing new products in order to grow. The product development process consists of a series of stages, which are outlined here. Figure 3.1 shows these stages.

1. **Idea Generation.** The first stage of product development involves conceiving of ideas for potential products. Large firms maintain research and development departments whose goal is to keep the firm competitive through the identification of potential new products or the modification of existing ones. R&D is especially vital in fast-moving high-tech industries that must remain on the cutting edge of technology in order to stay alive. Other sources of ideas within the company include executives, sales and service personnel, production workers, and marketing researchers. Ideas also come from external sources such as trade journals, competitors, and customers, and sometimes inventors approach companies with ideas for products.

Products can be totally new concepts, offshoots of other products, or improved versions of old products. Cable radio was born from cable television; new Cheerios are crispier to ward off sogginess; and new Wheaties have been developed with a milder, whole-grain flavor. Sometimes a new use for an old product can be marketed with positive results. Whether a product is considered new is a function of the individual consumer's perspective.

2. **Idea Screening.** Ideas must be evaluated in terms of the company's existing products, markets, and resources. Here are some of the questions that must be addressed:

- Will the product fit into the company's current product line?
- Can it be sold to existing customers, or must new markets be developed?

Figure 3.1 The Product Development Process

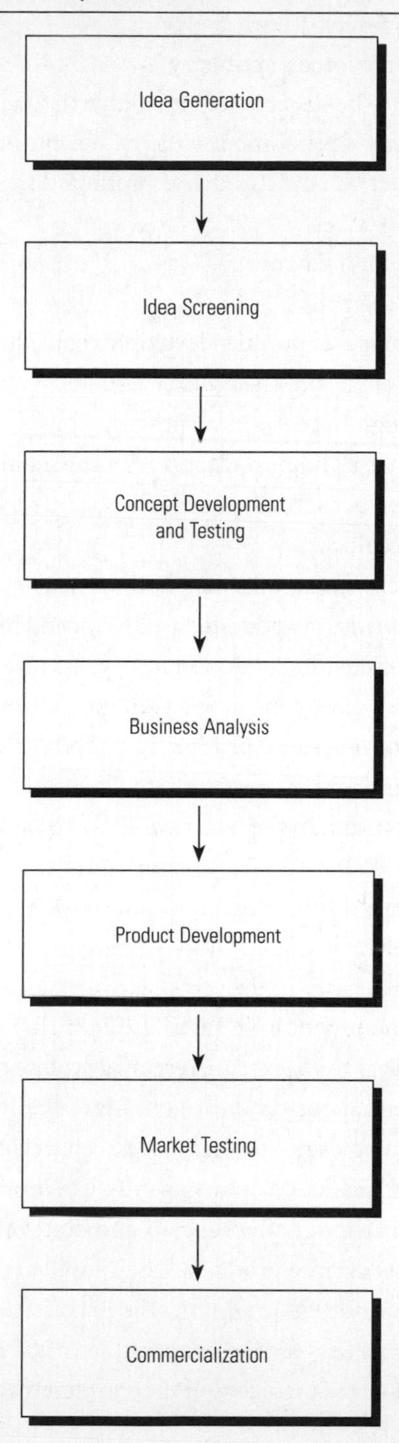

- Will additional personnel be required to develop the product?
- Must the sales force be retrained?
- Will plant expansion be necessary?
- Can the product be distributed through existing channels?
- How quickly can development costs be recaptured?
- Can the product be advertised and promoted through currently used media?
- Can it qualify for a patent?

Marketing managers and product developers consider many factors during the screening stage, but the basic consideration is whether potential profits will outweigh the costs. One potential pitfall of introducing new products into any existing product line is cannibalism, a situation in which the new product actually takes sales away from the organization's other existing products.

Pricing in today's economy has had an impact on new products. There is a trend toward producing quality products with fewer of the extra features that customers don't really value and offering them at a lower price. Instead of pricing products in the traditional way, by adding a profit margin to the cost of producing a product, companies are first setting a target price for a new product. Then the product is designed with that price in mind. In the fast-food industry, some companies have introduced items that are priced at a dollar or less, in order to appeal to younger consumers and to commuters who weigh the costs of a daily doughnut and coffee for each workday of the year.

3. **Concept Development and Testing.** Ideas that pass the screening process are turned over to marketing research professionals, who describe the concept to potential customers and analyze their reactions to it. Do they like it? Would it be useful to them? What characteristics of the product do they like and dislike? Would they buy it? How would they change it to make it better? Demographic, social, and cultural factors affect how consumers respond to certain products. Their input at this stage is valuable to product developers both in improving the product design and in identifying the strongest markets for the proposed product. From this research, a product concept emerges, which will then undergo a complex and stringent business analysis.

4. **Business Analysis.** Many products never go beyond the concept stage because, despite their merits, they would not provide the firm with enough profits to justify development costs. A demand analysis, or a forecast of market and sales potential, must be measured against a cost analysis that considers R&D, production, and marketing costs. Many variables will be considered, including the quality, pricing, and placement of any competition; the number of consumers who will likely be interested in buying the product; the economic conditions that may affect the consumers; any special requirements of the timing for getting the product to market; the cost of the conceptual development and the design, modeling, materials procurement, manufacturing needs, packaging, advertising, sales, storage and shipping; and many others, as needed by the individual market and product under review. In medium-sized to large companies, the product developer or product development manager will usually make a formal presentation of this analysis and proposal to the division or corporate management, including the top executive and operations, sales and marketing, manufacturing, and financial managers, and perhaps also the board of directors. If the product still looks good after this analysis, it enters the product development stage.

5. **Product Development.** Working together, the R&D and engineering departments develop a prototype or model of the product. Only if the prototype tests have the expected outcome in terms of performance, quality, and safety is the product then slated for market testing.

6. **Market Testing.** Conventional market testing is done in one or two sample locations, which are chosen because they represent the larger market for the product. Because of the high costs of this type of testing, companies sometimes hire outside research firms to run minimarket tests. For retail items, these companies arrange to have stores place the product on their shelves to see how consumers like it. Some tests are run in laboratories, where subjects are shown ads and promotion materials along with the product. Subjects are taken to mock or real stores, and researchers monitor their buying behavior. Computer analysis of the test results determines whether the product has been received as expected. If so, it enters the commercialization stage.

Despite elaborate testing, problems can arise after a product is introduced. For instance, before Unilever introduced a manganese-based detergent, fully sixty thousand consumers tested the product over a three-month period. Nevertheless, the company had to reformulate this powder to combat a charge from an independent consumer organization, which claimed that its own test showed that cotton clothes were weakened over time by the new detergent. Critics said that Unilever's tests were conducted over too short a period and with towels made of linen, a relatively tough fabric. Because of the chance of occurrences such as this, each stage in the product development process must be carefully thought out, if the product is to be successful.

7. **Commercialization.** This is the stage at which the marketing organization operates at full power to develop a marketing strategy for the life of the product. Activities involving personnel from production, distribution, sales, advertising, and promotion are coordinated as the product enters production. Technically, this last stage of product development is the first stage in the product life cycle. When sales of a product start to decline, the company often introduces a "new and improved" version.

Sometimes repositioning can revitalize the sale of a product. For example, after years of successful sales of its Pampers products, the Procter & Gamble Company introduced Pampers Phases, disposable diapers with different designs and absorbencies for four different stages of a child's early years. These diapers may be nearly the same as the "small," "medium," and "large" sizes in which Pampers have been sold for many years, but renaming the product to call attention to its relation to a child's growth stages attracted many new customers. Similarly, Kimberly-Clark has made absorbency improvements to such brands as Kotex, Kleenex, Cottonelle, and Huggies, resulting in increased market share and higher profits.

Implicit in the product life cycle is the continuing need for new products and new marketing strategies, as well as for the people who develop them.

THE IMPORTANCE OF BRANDS

Brands have traditionally played a lead role in the successful product offerings of companies, and they continue to do so. Marketers view successful brands as strategic assets. Brand names become successful when consumers associate them with tangible or intangible benefits that they receive from the products. Cheerios, Coca-Cola, Cover Girl, Eveready, Hershey, Snap-on, and Tide are examples of brand names that have become household words.

Depending on current fads, young consumers want toys, electronic devices, and clothes with certain labels. Brand names are used to suggest certain styles and qualities; they distinguish products from similar ones and often lend interest and excitement to promotion campaigns. Brand identification can help or hurt products. Logos denoting brand names have considerable image appeal, and a great logo can be a powerful advertising tool. For example, one of the most frequently requested tattoos in tattoo parlors across America is the Harley-Davidson logo. The key to selling a successful brand is the same as for any successful product: understanding its market.

Researchers involved in brand decisions endeavor to identify not only consumer preferences and satisfaction but also the feelings, emotions, and relationships that consumers associate with a particular brand. More companies in all industries are using the technology model developed in the 1990s, emphasizing teams, getting products out faster, using database information, and incorporating online marketing strategies in product development.

The brand manager's work encompasses how a product is developed, produced, sold, and serviced. Brands, especially high-tech brands, are built using specific characteristics, customer benefits, emotional rewards to customers, quality consistent with promises, and identification of the essential nature of the brand. Successful brand management rewards companies with what they seek most: loyal customers who are well understood by the company, a good relationship with suppliers and distributors through a promise of value, and customers' willingness to buy their products even at premium prices. For good examples, some of the most successful of the consumer electronics companies—Apple, Dell, IBM, and Hewlett-Packard—come immediately to mind. Much of the consumer market today is characterized by eroding product differences, which makes brand identification and loyalty even more important in purchasing decisions. Closely and continually tracking the ups and downs of customer purchases, feelings, and satisfaction is crucial to successful brand management.

BRAND INFORMATION ONLINE

Internet marketing has transformed the commercial world and has provided a previously unimagined scope of market segments. Numerous B2B (business-to-business) firms now offer brand managers news, trends, market data, customer information, and other relevant detail over the Internet, which in turn is used for marketing to consumers through traditional channels as well as via the Internet.

The global marketing firm Opinion Research Corporation International, in addition to offering its e-commerce customers information on brand awareness and shopper satisfaction, has launched an Internet survey to identify the most powerful online brands. The website Brandcities.com provides brand managers with a home page containing the latest best practices, industry news, analysis, and commentary by marketing experts. TalkCity Marketing Group offers online solutions to companies wanting to capitalize on the multibillion-dollar e-marketing sector in the areas of customer attraction, conversion, and retention.

Nielsen/NetRatings, a global leader in Internet media and market research, empowers brand managers with specialized consumer profile reports and online audience measurement to help them identify the best websites to reach a brand's key consumers.

Brand managers need help not only in reaching consumers with their products but also in reaching distributors and franchisees with their advertising messages. BrandMuscle enables manufacturers to set up a system online that allows their distributors and franchisees to customize their ads by selecting from preapproved images, coupons, and customer locations rather than risking a distortion of the manufacturer's message by coming up with their own methods of promotion.

Another company, Connecting Dots, provides domain name resources as well as intellectual property resources and consulting and educational services. Brand Fidelity and Name Protect are examples of naming-related firms.

The power of online information and promotion of products for all types of companies, not only Internet companies, is being harnessed more every day around the globe. Specific online companies will come and go, but the opportunities offered over the Web will continue to expand and be a potent part of marketing well into the future.

RELATED WORK OF PRODUCT AND BRAND MANAGERS

The product or brand manager is assigned a product or product line that is approved for development. Determining objectives and marketing strategies for the product is part of the job description but falls short of describing the work that these managers must perform. Since product managers have no direct authority over personnel in other departments on which they depend for their success, such as advertising or sales, they must be skilled in gaining the cooperation and support of colleagues. It is not unusual for companies to sell products that compete with one another. In this case, a product manager must vie with other product managers within the firm for this cooperation and the necessary resources.

Product managers may be assigned to manage a product through its entire life cycle. Sometimes, however, a new-product development manager is assigned only for a product's initial development and test marketing. At the conclusion of test marketing, a product manager will take over and remain in charge of the product throughout the rest of its life cycle. Working under the marketing manager, a product manager must provide the information necessary for top-level management decisions. The responsibilities of product managers are as follows:

- Evaluate product testing and recommend whether to terminate development, modify the product, or begin the campaign
- Work with production development team, plan the introduction and scheduling of the finished product and packaging
- Provide information and recommendations on product pricing in cooperation with the marketing research department
- Develop sales and profitability forecasts and marketing budgets with the finance department
- Analyze statistics and recommendations from marketing research to allocate funding for advertising and promotion campaigns

• Identify channels of distribution, such as wholesalers, retailers, or direct sales to the public

• Work with marketing research and the advertising agency to position the product—that is, create an image of the product in the minds of consumers as having the attributes that are desired

• Coordinate production and promotion of the product from start to finish

PRODUCT RECALLS

A less savory role in product management involves recalling products that have already been distributed or sold because they pose threats or hazards to consumers. In such cases, usually a product recall manager is assigned to reverse the marketing channels in the distribution process. Stock is removed from retail shelves and distribution warehouses, returned to the manufacturer, and either repaired or disposed of. The product recall manager must analyze, plan, budget, organize, communicate, and oversee this entire operation, which often entails working under severe pressure and in close cooperation with the public relations, legal, and other departments of the organization.

PRODUCT MANAGEMENT TEAMS

The product manager typically has an assistant product manager to help in overseeing and coordinating all activities associated with the product throughout the development process and life cycle. Often the manager and assistant manager head up a product management team consisting of specialists from all areas, including marketing research, R&D, production, advertising, sales promotion, and sales. Sometimes managers choose their own teams; other times, specialists from various areas who share an interest in a particular product volunteer to develop that product. Outside specialists are sometimes called in to support this effort.

Product and brand managers should possess a high degree of creativity and knowledge, widespread interests, and consumer awareness. Good managers try to foster an environment that is conducive to creativity, in which each team member feels equal and comfortable taking a role in brainstorming and offering ideas. Ideally, top management is committed to using whatever resources are necessary to get the job done efficiently and effectively. For this reason, there are no rigid, set formulas for personnel deployment. Rather, personnel assignments may vary from project to project, as the situation requires.

As a product goes into development, product managers and their assistants interact with almost every department in the company. This exposure provides excellent opportunities for learning every aspect of the company business and making contacts that could be useful in advancing to higher positions.

PACKAGING, DISTRIBUTION, AND PROMOTION

Three important aspects of product development that are often planned and carried out with the help of additional in-house or outside specialists are packaging, distribution, and promotion.

Packaging

Packaging is sometimes an unheralded aspect of the marketing process, yet it is as carefully planned as the product itself. A package does more than contain and protect the contents of a product throughout distribution. A package also advertises and promotes the product. Clever packages can give an advantage to one product over a competing one. In addition to being convenient and attractive, a package can be functional; examples include squeeze bottles for margarine, mustard, and ketchup; resealable plastic bags for cheeses and cold cuts; and attractive tin or plastic containers that can be reused.

The smart product manager enlists package designers as part of the development team at the beginning of the project. Engineers and graphic designers generate ideas for packaging with suggestions from other team members, including advertising and promotion specialists. Packages may be produced in-house or be modeled by, produced by, and purchased from outside companies according to specifications provided by in-house designers and other team members.

Distribution

Getting a product into the hands of the consumer is fundamental to the marketing effort. A small bakery sells directly to consumers, but what about a large bakery? And how do bakeries get the supplies needed to produce their products? Manufacturers get the materials needed for production from suppliers. Their completed products are usually sent to intermediaries, also called resellers or middlemen. These intermediaries, whether individuals or large firms, may be retailers or wholesalers. In this process, called "two-step distribution," they serve as a link between the manufacturer and the final buyers of the product. Careers in retailing and wholesaling are further described in Chapters 6 and 7. Producers, intermediaries, and final buyers form what is called a "marketing channel" or "channel of distribution."

Distribution involves a host of marketing functions, including transporting and storing (warehousing) products and supplying market information. Since profits depend on the secure, efficient, and effective delivery of products into the hands of consumers, distribution is thoroughly planned as an aspect of product development. As mentioned in the discussion of idea screening, having channels of distribution in place is a big plus for any new product. Product or brand managers plan distribution strategy as part of the overall marketing strategy. This strategy is then implemented by respective distribution professionals, beginning at the top with the distribution manager and including warehouse managers, traffic control managers, traffic auditors, shipping and transportation managers, and the workers who support all these functions. For products with special needs, it may include heating and refrigeration handlers and managers, safety officers, inspectors, customs and duties managers, and transportation contractors, among others.

Promotion

The product manager works with a variety of specialists to best determine how to launch the new product on the market. There are four elements of promotion:

- Advertising
- Sales Promotion
- Public Relations
- Personal Selling

The extent to which these elements are used depends on the industry and the product. Careers in these areas are described in Chapters 4 through 7.

OPPORTUNITIES IN PRODUCT MANAGEMENT

Carrying out the duties of product management is much like running a small business. For this reason, most companies assign entrepreneurial types to the job. In fact, product managers sometimes go on to use their corporate experience to start their own businesses. Large manufacturers often hire only M.B.A.s for entry-level positions in product management, usually as assistant product manager. More opportunities in product management in smaller companies are available to promising candidates with undergraduate degrees. Many of the largest companies provide formal training programs; others have more informal training, and in smaller companies, training is often done "on the job."

Promotion from assistant to product manager is the usual career track. Some companies that produce dozens of brands in various categories have created a higher managerial position, called category manager, to whom all brand or product managers in that category report. The category manager, who reports to the marketing manager, has the responsibility of determining marketing strategy for all brands in that product category. Promotions from product management, which is middle-level management, to top management are possible. Corporate marketing management is discussed in Chapter 8.

According to the 2007–2008 edition of the *Occupational Outlook Handbook*, published by the U.S. Department of Labor, the broad category of managerial jobs, including sales and marketing, public relations, and promotions managers, totaled approximately 582,000 jobs in 2007. The category is expected to grow by about 12 percent, or nearly as fast as average, through 2016. Though it is impossible to know how many of these jobs will be for product managers, expected growth in this category is relatively good, with many of these new jobs coming in the computer, electronics, and Internet industries. Brand managers are counted within the broad category of advertising, marketing, promotions, public relations, and sales managers.

The *Occupational Outlook Handbook* states that median annual earnings in May 2006 were $73,060 for advertising and promotions managers, $98,720 for marketing managers, $91,560 for sales managers, and $82,180 for public relations managers.

Salaries of product and brand managers are affected by the importance of the product and brand to which managers are assigned. The larger the amount of company resources budgeted for product development, the more important the role of the product manager and the higher the salary. Salaries vary from industry to industry as well. Other factors that affect salaries and components of compensation packages for managers are discussed in Chapters 8 and 11. The best chance of landing the most desirable position is to find an internship or cooperative program while still in college. This experience can often lead to excellent job opportunities in all areas of marketing.

ADDITIONAL SOURCES OF INFORMATION

The best sources of information on career planning in the field of product management are professional associations. Some of these follow:

American Management Association
1601 Broadway
New York, NY 10019
amanet.org

Institute of Brand Science
Goizueta Business School
Emory University
1300 Clifton Rd.
Atlanta, GA 30322
emorymi.com

Product Development and Management Association
15000 Commerce Pkwy., Ste. C
Mount Laurel, NJ 08054
pdma.org

Project Management Institute
PMI Global Operations Center
4 Campus Blvd.
Newton Square, PA 19073
pmi.org

CHAPTER 4

CAREERS IN ADVERTISING AND SALES PROMOTION

Madison Avenue's advertising and sales promotion image of glamour mixed with ambition, energy, drive, and perhaps a bit of conniving has been fostered by movies and television for decades. Not all advertising and sales promotion jobs fit that representation, but the pulse of the industry can be intensely felt by thousands of people whose daily work lives are much like that Hollywood conception.

THE TRADITIONAL IMAGE

As a recent example, you may be familiar with the role played by Mel Gibson in the film *What Women Want*, in which the protagonist suddenly gains the ability to read women's minds. Nike, just at the time that film was to be made, was ready to launch a major line of women's shoes and apparel, and the corporation was happy to have its product highlighted in the film. Another illustrative novel and film, *The Man in the Gray Flannel Suit*, portrayed an image of the Madison Avenue ad man of the 1950s that became famous. Often movie and TV "bad guys" aren't really so bad and turn into likable human beings by the end of the show. Industry insiders have said that David Clennon's portrayal of ad agency executive Miles Drentell on the TV show *thirtysomething* was among the most accurate they had seen.

CHANGING SPEED—FROM FAST TO WARP

In reality, the field of advertising has always been highly competitive, stressful, and results oriented, and its fast-paced world has actually been portrayed fairly effectively by the entertainment industry. That pace has quickened over the years. With the growth of the vast, instant communication provided by the Internet, the world of advertising and promotion has geared up proportionally.

The stresses of intense and hard-driving competition, the constant need for success in promoting sales, looming deadlines for various kinds of publications and product presentations, and the day-to-day concerns of working with others who are also under substantial pressure make advertising and sales promotion a career area for people who are physically, mentally, and neurologically hardy and well balanced.

Rapid change takes place in this field as competitors continually strive for advantage. Promoting products through new advertising and sales promotion channels is evolving fast as technology opens new avenues to reach consumers. Advertising has undergone major changes and has taken increasing and ongoing advantage of these new opportunities to reach consumers via the Internet and many other technologies such as cell phones, BlackBerries, and MP3 players.

Advertising, technology, and marketing experts use approaches such as infomercials that target specific consumer groups; advertising more at live events where consumers are a captive audience; revising use of both unconventional media, such as in-store advertising, and conventional media, such as newspapers, magazines, and radio; and selling directly to consumers using new media.

Then there's viral marketing—a technique in which a message placed at the bottom of an e-mail, or tacked onto an offer passed along by users, spreads like the flu. Hotmail, a free e-mail service, put the message "Get your free e-mail at Hotmail.com" at the bottom of each e-mail and acquired eleven million users in eighteen months. To encourage referrals, some companies offer incentives such as discounts on services and free merchandise. Along these lines, Spotcast Communications offered its customers free airtime on their cell phones in exchange for listening to brief phone ads at the start of a call. Sales promotion campaigns subtly and effectively influence the American consumer to purchase certain items.

A company's product-promotion efforts may include any or all of the following components:

- Advertising
- Sales Promotion
- Personal Selling
- Public Relations

How much time and money is spent on each of these components will depend on the product itself and on detailed analyses and decisions made by management.

RELATIONSHIP OF ADVERTISING AND SALES PROMOTION

Advertising and sales promotion work together to win customers. Often commercials advertise promotions. The distinction between advertising and sales promotion is that advertising *suggests*, while promotion *motivates*. Obviously some ads do both. Signs that say, "Buy one, get one free" or coupons that specify, "Save 55 cents" are used to motivate consumers to try a particular product. While advertising may go on for indefinite periods, sales promotion is planned for a limited time, usually when a product is first introduced. Thus the frequent announcement of "Special Promotion!" Often packaged-goods companies spend more dollars on consumer promotions than on media advertising. Giveaways, tie-ins, coupons, and contests are in keeping with the trend of selling to individuals rather than the masses. Each of these campaigns will be researched, planned, designed, developed, and produced by a team of specialists.

THE EVOLUTION OF ADVERTISING

A capsule review of the history of advertising shows how much the field has changed—and how much it has changed the world—over the years.

Way back in 1878, long before the existence of modern advertising and communications, three small but defining events occurred:

• First, a worker churned a batch of White Soap too long, making it light enough to float.

• Second, an analysis showed the soap to be 99.44 percent pure.

• Finally, Harley Procter sat in church one Sunday musing over the words of the Forty-Fifth Psalm, "All thy garments smell of myrrh and aloes and cassia out of ivory palaces, whereby they have made thee glad."

On Monday, Harley Procter changed the name of his soap from White Soap to Ivory Soap. The following ad blitz carried a now familiar message—"Ivory soap. It floats." Thus was a brand created out of a commodity, boosting a nice little soap business into the giant soap empire that eventually became Procter & Gamble. This story and many others just as engaging are told in the book *Advertising in America: The First 200 Years* by Charles Goodrum and Helen Dalrymple.

Early advertising established the ground rules for advertisements that still exist to this day. However, unlike the early ads, which communicated a basic selling message in an inventive but forthright manner, the ads of today use more daring techniques, to avoid being lost in the barrage of media noise. As a result, some artistically exciting ads sometimes leave viewers asking themselves, "What are they selling?"

The goal of every successful ad is to make a creative impact and sell the product. Ads that do not result in sales are failures. Even the ads we love sometimes fail to deliver on their objective. Recall Taco Bell's "Chihuahua" ad campaign. While it generated $155 million from the incidental sales of the promotional "talking Chihuahua" toy dogs and related merchandise, which charmed the public, it failed completely to boost Taco Bell's sagging food sales. After all the effort and expense of the enormous campaign, the company was back to square one when it came to bolstering its regular product sales.

Creative types who opt for advertising as a career must have a reliable business orientation and be able to take accurate aim, successfully targeting the sales results that their jobs require.

ADVERTISING STRATEGY

In 2007, advertisers spent more than $2.6 million for thirty seconds of ad time during the Super Bowl, generating ad revenues of hundreds of millions of dollars. The ten most-watched television programs in history comprise seven Super Bowls, two Winter Olympics broadcasts, and the famous February 28, 1983, finale of the popular show "MASH."

When the goal is to reach the greatest number of potential consumers at one time, ad spots during the Super Bowl are a safe bet. The quality and provocative nature of these ads are so high that the spots are talked about after the broadcast almost as much as the game itself.

The trend in advertising today, however, is toward textbook-type advertising that stresses value and distinguishes a product from its rivals. This is true even for Apple Computer, whose dramatic, costly, high-concept ads of the early 1980s, designed to produce images linking the product to the customer, made advertising history. In leaner times, companies are more likely to take a safe approach than to risk many thousands, or millions, of advertising dollars on radical new concepts. This is not to suggest that creative visual artists will be unable to "do their thing" in advertising. The art director today still wields more clout than his or her counterpart in copywriting.

An effective advertising strategy is critical to the successful launch of new products. Basically, advertising involves creating information designed to increase sales and placing it in mass media such as the Internet, television, radio, newspapers, magazines, and billboards.

The total advertising effort to introduce a product, or stimulate additional sales of an existing product, is called an advertising campaign and features numerous professionals working in a variety of capacities. Often considered the glamour job of marketing, advertising is in fact highly competitive and very hard work. However, for creative individuals who can stand the pressure, the work can be exciting, challenging, and rewarding.

WHERE ADVERTISING PROFESSIONALS ARE EMPLOYED

Advertising professionals find jobs in advertising agencies, in advertising departments of large companies (in-house advertising agencies), or with mass media as advertising sales representatives. Functions performed are similar in the first two venues, the obvious difference being that ad agencies promote products for client companies who pay for their services, while in-house agencies promote the company's own products. Both aim for success. The agency that does not come up with a successful ad campaign for a client loses the account, and the advertising professionals involved in unsuccessful campaigns sometimes lose their jobs.

Most major ad campaigns are created in advertising agencies. One-third of the ad agencies are large, employing more than a thousand people. The other two-thirds are small and often specialize in serving particular industries or market niches. The vast majority of advertising jobs are in independent agencies. In-house agencies offer positions that are comparable in both responsibility and salary, and creative jobs in companies are often less competitive, and perhaps slightly less stressful, than in agencies.

A position often found in large companies that sell goods and services is the marketing communications specialist. Supervised by marketing managers, these specialists act as the liaison between their company and outside firms engaged to support marketing efforts such as advertising, sales promotion, and public relations firms. They articulate the company's product strategies and requirements to these firms and report progress and queries on campaigns to the marketing manager. In addition, they may have responsibilities for internal communications.

CAREERS IN ADVERTISING AGENCIES

Advertising agencies usually have at least four main departments:

- Account Services
- Research
- Creative
- Media

Jobs in advertising agencies are divided equally between two groups:

- **Account support professionals.** The "suits" deal with clients as well as in-house departments, including account services, marketing research, and media planning.
- **Creative-function professionals.** The "creatives" design, write, draw, do layouts, sometimes work all night to get the presentations ready, and may be able to dress in jeans and sweats in some agencies and corporate departments.

Advancement into account services comes with experience and success in one of the other departments and can lead to management.

The Account Services Department

Just as the product manager oversees every aspect of product development, the account executive plans and monitors all activities in an ad campaign. The proverbial buck stops with the account executive, who bears overall responsibility, although all jobs are vulnerable when major ad campaigns are involved. As noted earlier, an unsuccessful advertising campaign can result in a product failure for the client and the loss of a major customer for the agency. Because of the make-or-break nature of the work in account services, only experienced individuals need apply. Account executives may be promoted from other areas in the agency or hired from other advertising agencies.

The account executive works with the client—an individual or a company—in planning an advertising campaign. To assess the client's advertising needs, the account executive must be familiar with all of the client's marketing efforts and how the ad campaign should fit in. Communicating the requirements and preferences to the creative and media departments and coordinating all activities related to the account is the responsibility of the account executive.

The account coordinator or traffic manager is another core member of the account services staff. This individual tracks and coordinates the work of all four departments throughout the advertising campaign, communicating timetables and monitoring progress. He or she must make sure that all pieces of information, plans, completed work, and changes in plans, if any, are coordinated and communicated to each person involved and that the work flow does not stop.

A trainee in account services, the assistant account executive, usually has experience in advertising and a college degree. Entry-level duties might include handling inquires from clients and other departments, monitoring progress and deadlines in the creative department, communicating with the traffic manager on schedules and ad spots, and in general assisting the account executive. Advancement to account executive may occur after one or two successful years as an assistant. Initially, account executives handle only smaller accounts. They meet with clients to plan a strategy and with other departments to see that it is implemented. They accept or reject ideas from the creative department, and they determine media and ad schedules according to the client's budget.

An assistant account executive who successfully handles ad campaigns and works effectively with clients can expect to be promoted to senior account executive. Senior account executives work on larger accounts and may oversee and advise other account executives, thus gaining the opportunity to hone their administrative skills.

The chief position in account services is that of the accounts supervisor or accounts manager. Managers not only oversee accounts but also actively solicit new clients and advise and train sales staff. These managers are instrumental in bringing new business into the agency and assigning accounts to executives. Acquiring and keeping accounts is what makes ad agencies successful.

The Research Department

Information collected through consumer research and product testing is often the basis for an ad campaign, because it identifies potential users of the product and the reasons why the product should appeal to this particular market. The research department of an advertising agency functions much like the marketing research department of any company, but the focus is, of course, on effective advertising.

Monitoring trends is a principal function in that trends can determine how products are positioned in their markets. For example, the nation's divorce rate is edging lower as baby boomers reach middle age. In response, it is likely that more ads will focus on families using products.

An entry-level job as a research project director usually requires a college or graduate degree, plus experience in advertising or marketing research. Research in an advertising agency means collecting information on how consumers perceive particular products. Conducting primary research involves the development of surveys, usually conducted by outside firms, and the analysis of survey results. Writing reports containing this analysis, along with additional information gathered from secondary sources such as the government or trade groups, is the job of the research project director. Account services, the creative department, and the media department use these reports in planning the advertising campaign.

Once the campaign begins, research focuses on its effects on the intended audience, and changes may be recommended. Promotion from research project director to research account executive depends on talent, innovation, and reliability. Devising new methods of product and market testing and recommending successful advertising strategies are essential to moving up in the research department.

In large organizations, several years of successful experience should lead to the position of associate research director, and then advertising research director, and finally research department manager. As in all departments in businesses, advancement involves taking on more supervisory and administrative duties. Administrative skills are universally useful, so movement from one department to another is not unusual, particularly for people with a background in research in which problem solving and data analysis are requisite skills.

The Creative Department

Most of the advertising jobs are in the creative department, which is composed of copywriters, graphic artists, and layout workers who work in teams under the art director and the copy chief.

The creative team synthesizes information from the research department, the account executive, and the client to develop the advertisements that will attract the targeted consumers to the client's product. Graphic designers and copywriters are essentially problem solvers, creating distinctive and innovative solutions to the problem of how best to attract and hold the attention of a specific group of people and persuade those people to buy what they are selling, whether it's a product, a service, or a statement of principles and philosophy.

It is hard to capture the attention of today's Web-surfing, channel-surfing, and BlackBerry-flipping public, so art directors are experimenting with every available tool, including interactive and multimedia e-commerce ads; in-your-face graphics; and bold and outsize, florescent-art fonts. Letters leap out of ads and commercials; different typefaces are combined; sentences swim off in all directions. Computers make it easy to create special effects in typestyles, but surveys point out that if the message is hard to read, consumers usually ignore it. Some U.S. ad agencies incorporate the position of type director or type designer, also used in British agencies, to keep type designs fresh and interesting as well as legible.

Advertising is a lot more than catchy phrases, gimmicky slogans, and novelty art. Cleverness and originality are certainly a part of what is required for creative advertising professionals, and humor can be a compelling sales tool as well, but the advertising professional is required to have solid skills and effective methods.

Sometimes advertising is used to change a product's image and reposition the product to attract a broader range of consumers. Xerox, which many consumers perceived as strictly a copier manufacturer due to strong brand identification, launched an ad campaign, "Putting It Together," that focused on the document, to convey that its products can now compute, scan, fax, copy, collate, and bind—representing the ultimate in document-producing machines.

Celebrity spokespersons are often used by ad campaigns to convey their advertising message both directly and indirectly. Sports marketers estimate that Lance Armstrong, seven-time Tour de France winner and cancer survivor, has a product endorsement portfolio worth many millions of dollars a year from a variety of companies.

Consider the advertising value to Nike of having a tennis player win the U.S. Open wearing Nike products from head to toe. As part of their contracts, athletes are paid to wear company insignias or logos. Advertisers are capitalizing on the public's desire to identify with celebrities by using products they promote. Stars are well compensated for helping a company sell its products. One of the most important considerations in advertising is the target audience—those who will buy the products that are advertised.

The Media Department

Once ads are created, they are positioned in one or more of the most appropriate media, selected for the broadest impact. Media professionals develop a media strategy—the proper media mix for best promoting the product. This involves defining the target audience, where they live, and how they can best be reached. Using information from the research department and computer databases, media planners try to reach the largest number of potential customers in the most cost-effective way.

Internet advertising has mushroomed in recent years and is capable of reaching millions of users more economically than most print or television ad forms. In addition, cookies implanted in consumers' computers have enabled customer research to be conducted on a previously unimagined scale. Advertisers can access information about consumer viewing and buying habits across continents or internationally.

Declines in both broadcast network viewing and publications subscriptions combined with rising print and television ad prices have also spurred marketers to examine alternate media such as cable television and the thousands of new special-interest publications that have arisen. Basic cable networks offer a highly targeted and upscale audience to advertisers at lower prices than the major networks. Regional sports cable networks have been big advertising winners, with ad revenues rising every year.

Marketers have concluded that targeted messages through specialized media are economical and effective. Advertisers want ads that are addressed to targeted age, income, psychology, and buying patterns placed in media that target those specific groups. The desired media packages may include combinations of magazines, television programs, books, and videotapes. Technology has produced still other advertising media. Sony Corporation, for example, erected a 23.5′ × 32′ outdoor color video display in Times Square in New York, showing ads, news, and public service announcements. Internet providers such as America Online and CompuServe run ads along with information. In-store advertising in groceries and other retail stores has gone from ads on flyers, shopping carts, and checkout dividers to television sets mounted over the checkout counter running various ads. All in all, the field of media planning is becoming more complex and challenging.

Candidates for positions in media planning are chosen for their analytical and statistical skills, as well as the ability to accept high levels of responsibility. College graduates typically enter the media department as assistant media planners.

Working under experienced planners, beginners are involved in computation and analysis of numbers provided by research or audience ratings done by outside sources such as Nielsen. Advancement to the position of media planner brings far more responsibility.

Media planners work closely with account services and sometimes directly with clients in determining the best media mix—how much television, magazine, or other coverage to use. Choosing from many options makes this a challenging job. Adding to the challenge is the need to adhere to the client's media budget, although the media group will usually have made detailed recommendations to the client regarding budget before the project is begun, and these will have been agreed upon, so that appropriate funds are available.

Once a client accepts the media plan, media professionals meet with advertising sales representatives from various media and begin evaluating proposals. Negotiating contracts for print or Internet advertising space or airtime according to the media plan is the next step. This may be done by media directors and their associates or, in larger agencies, by regional or national spot buyers skilled in negotiations of this type. After five to ten years of experience, media directors can advance to media planners. The media manager, who is in charge of both planning and buying, holds the top job in media.

Media sales reps usually enter the field from positions in media planning, sometimes as spot buyers. Most sales reps work on straight or part commission and therefore have considerable earning potential. Media sales is high-pressure work, and stress is a factor that should be evaluated by prospective job seekers. Positions in sales are reviewed in more detail in Chapters 6 and 7.

Along with strong quantitative skills, media professionals must possess strong communications and interpersonal skills. Functioning as part of a team and acquiescing to clients' wishes and to directives from the internal account services management require an ability to work well with others and a willingness to compromise. The cost of media is the big-budget item in advertising. Consequently, the pressures and demands on the media department are extreme. However, media is a well-traveled avenue into account services.

TRUTH IN ADVERTISING

Truth-in-advertising laws to prevent misleading ads have been passed in all of the United States and in most developed countries. Unfortunately, they do not protect consumers all of the time. Some companies continue to defy the law and run misleading ads for products that may cheat or have other harmful impacts on consumers.

In recent years, serious damage has been done in some cases by misleading and confusing advertising, especially within certain industries. Major lawsuits have been brought against some food product, financial, medical, and transportation industry corporations, among others, after consumers sustained significant harm from being misled. Truth in advertising means truth—not half-truths—as some advertisers have been forced to acknowledge the hard way.

Not all misleading ads are created with words. As a case in point, the Hot Rod Association took strong exception to an ad showing a monster truck rolling over five cars and crushing all but one of them. The manufacturer of that car, which had run the ad, admitted to reinforcing the roof of that particular automobile with lumber and steel especially for the stunt.

As more commercials attack competing products by name, some of the maligned companies are charging that network review systems are allowing false ads on the air. Advertising industry ethics have often been questioned in the past, and the problem of misleading advertising is unlikely to disappear, especially during hard economic times.

As in every other industry, each person in advertising and promotion has the responsibility for ethical work. If a superior or a client in any project asks an employee to fake statistics, field trials, testimonials, or any other substantive aspect of the content of product advertisements or collateral marketing pieces, it is up to the employee to take a stand.

In selecting companies as potential employers, you should do thorough research on their histories. If you discover that lawsuits have been filed against a company for false or misleading advertising, you may want to continue your job search somewhere else.

JOB REQUIREMENTS AND CAREER PATHS

Usually a college degree and, especially important, a good representative portfolio of writing or art/design samples and ideas are required for breaking into this highly competitive area. Excellent verbal and visual communication skills, well-grounded computer skills, and familiarity with state-of-the-art hardware and software are essential. Familiarity with a breadth of advertising trends and media is also necessary.

Once hired as a junior copywriter, an individual might do everything from answering the telephone to taking part in creative brainstorming sessions. The sources of creativity and the formation of ideas remain a mystery; this combination of knowledge and imagination can neither be learned nor predicted. The ability to see things in new ways is a prerequisite in creative work.

A junior copywriter usually works under the supervision of an experienced copywriter for a period of training. Once promoted to copywriter, he or she is responsible for writing ad copy, developing concepts for campaigns, and teaming with artists and layout workers to present finished ads and ideas for commercials. Copywriters must be able to work under tight deadlines, ensure that their writing is absolutely factual and accurate, demonstrate good writing skills and creative imagination, subordinate their egos to the needs of the overall campaigns, and tolerate last-minute changes under pressure.

Artists, illustrators, designers, animators, and layout artists work under an art director to create the visual impact of an ad campaign or of single ads by executing the computer designs, planning storyboards, designing computer interactions and animation sequences, selecting photographs, drawing illustrations, choosing print size and type, or sketching scenes for print media ads, videos, websites, and television commercials. In addition to preparing print, Internet, and television layouts, they design packages and create corporate images by planning, coordinating, and designing logos, trademarks, and various kinds of other symbols used for corporate and product identity.

Production managers oversee the actual printing and posting of ads, filming of commercials, or recording of radio spots.

Job advancement depends on performance. Producing good ads that sell products and make clients happy counts more than years of experience. As in sales, what you produce forms the basis on which you are evaluated. Senior copywriters are assigned the large national accounts that increase the agency's reputation and profits. Copy chiefs supervise other copywriters and work closely with media and account executives in developing ad campaign strategies. Promotions to senior copywriter and then to copy chief are contingent on talent and success.

TYPES OF SALES PROMOTION

Three types of sales promotions contribute to the overall promotion effort:

- Trade Promotions
- Sales Force Promotions
- Consumer Promotions

Trade promotions are geared toward intermediaries such as retailers. Manufacturers motivate intermediaries to carry their products by offering such incentives as free goods, dealer sales contests, trade show appearances, and paid cooperative ads. Both manufacturers and retailers offer *sales force promotions*, including sales meetings, contests, and bonuses. The final push to sell the product is through *consumer promotions*, which include samples, coupons, trading stamps, rebates, point-of-purchase displays, exhibits, brochures, catalogs, sweepstakes, contests, and gifts with purchase. Shampoo with free conditioner, prizes inside cereal boxes, plastic dishes with the dog food, and an infinite number of other promotions are used to motivate consumers to buy certain products. Low-cost marketing tools such as imprinted pens and pencils, magnets, and key chains function as miniature billboards. Some current in-store marketing techniques that show promise are electronic kiosks, frequent-shopper programs, floor signage, interactive displays, and video.

Some companies use contests to promote their products. Wisconsin-based Puffs sponsored a Tissue Box Design Contest for elementary school students, with the theme "What I Like Best About School." The grand-prize winner received a $25,000 savings bond for college and a personal computer for home and another for the classroom; additional winners from three different grade levels also received personal computers.

Sweepstakes, commonly used by soft drink companies and fast-food restaurants, can help to revitalize brands. Earthgrains enclosed game pieces in packages of its Break Cake snack cakes to be mailed in to the company for the chance of winning $50,000 or a consolation prize of a Break Cake T-shirt.

Often an upbeat, "try-it-you'll-like-it" tone of sales promotion helps to launch new products. A company must succeed in motivating a group of consumers to try a product before that product can be market tested. If testing reveals that the product is well received, the company may want to intensify promotion efforts to ensure that it has a winner. The power of promotion efforts and their importance to the success of products cannot be overestimated. Unless companies can stimulate consumers to try new products, even products with the best potential will be destined to fail, because bottom-line profits determine which products will continue to be sold.

POSITIONS IN SALES PROMOTION

The foregoing descriptions of advertising jobs are also largely descriptive of jobs in sales promotion, and many positions are similar in these two closely related areas. Sales promotion professionals may work for manufacturers, wholesalers, retailers, or sales promotion agencies that operate roughly the same way as advertising agencies.

A sales promotion specialist may participate in product development, both in learning about the product and in suggesting ways to launch it.

Sales promotion is highly specialized and not for beginners. Because of its importance and cost, sales promotion professionals enter the field with considerable knowledge in media, markets, computer design, graphic arts, technical tools, and marketing. Most commonly, sales promotion professionals have worked in either advertising or sales prior to entering the field.

Creativity is important in designing sales promotion campaigns. Coming up with something new and catchy that attracts consumers to the product is a challenge in a consumer society that is constantly bombarded by new products and promises. Demonstrators and models present the product to the public through Internet, television, and print promotions; in shopping malls and grocery stores; and at trade shows. Graphic artists and copywriters work together to produce packaging for samples, coupons, buttons, T-shirts, and other promotional items. Layouts, materials, sizes, and shapes are all part of the creative process. Sales promotion efforts are planned and coordinated by a specialist assigned to the product.

Just as an account executive in an advertising agency works with a client, a sales promotion specialist works with a promotion client. That client may be the representative of a large manufacturer or a single individual with a unique property who seeks expertise in promoting it.

Herb Ahrend, owner of the long-established Madison Avenue advertising and promotion agency Ahrend Associates, once described a typical day by saying it was *never* typical. He might meet in the morning with a major publishing executive who had suddenly acquired a line of books that were completely different from any others that the company sold. He might lunch with the recent heir of a European estate who now held a private collection of priceless Renaissance drawings never before seen by the public. After lunch, he might spend the rest of the afternoon considering the needs of a hopeful inventor of sports gear to fit the feet—an invention like short skis, which could be called "ski-skates." All three of the day's potential clients would have voiced the same question: "How can I sell this?" Markets, appeals, competition, viability, timing, budgets, goals, and more would have been given an overview, and the first sketch of ideas and planning would begin to take form.

Based on the client's product, sales promotion budget, and marketing research conducted both for the specific product and for similar products, a sales promotion specialist plans a campaign and directs a creative team in producing the activities, schedule, and items needed to carry out the plan. A good specialist possesses intelligence, excellent communicative skills, research and analytical abilities, administrative skills, market knowledge, fiscal responsibility, good timing, and the ability to coordinate multiple facets of a project, and—last but not least—talent, creativity, and unfailing "feel for the market."

ONLINE ADVERTISING AND PROMOTION

Nearly $10 billion in revenue accrued to the Internet advertising industry in the first half of 2007, for a 27 percent increase over the first half of 2006. Major Internet ad companies such as Google and Yahoo showed good returns. In the Internet, the advertising and promotion industry has a medium that is faster and cheaper, reaches many more people, and is more flexible, compared with other media, so that advertising and promotion can be finely tuned and directed to the most likely consumers of the product.

Marketers today can accomplish a wide variety of tasks online, including narrowly targeting advertising; distributing and tracking coupons; accessing information on agencies, designers, and advertising campaigns; and exploring career opportunities in their fields. Some methods commonly used for online advertising are e-mail ads, which target specific customers and have the best response rate; banners, which comprise a significant percentage of online ad revenue; skyscrapers, the skinny ads that run down the right or left side of a website and whose click rates can be seven times that of banners; streaming video and audio, in which ads are inserted into music and video clips as consumers view them like TV; effectiveness tracking, which places tiny files called cookies on viewers' computers, enabling the tracking of consumer behavior after ads are viewed; and minisites, pop-ups, and interstitials, which feature ads that burst onto screens without sending users to different sites.

More and more companies are offering consumers user-friendly, one-on-one, interactive websites to build brands and customer loyalty.

EXPANDING RANGE OF E-CHANNELS

E-channels are expanding, too. Advertisers have a range of choices for investing their media dollars, including Internet advertising, e-mail advertising, interactive TV, mobile communications, and electronic games.

Branding expert Martin Lindstrom has written in *Marketing Digest* that the potential of ad placements in gaming venues is expanding to tremendous proportions. With hundreds of millions of people taking an active part in the games industry every day, its potential is just waiting to be imaginatively used. Its advantages as an interactive medium, he emphasized, include the potential for product placement and strategies within the games and stories themselves, where players can select their gaming clothing and equipment, weapons, and trophies from advertisers' imbedded brands.

In 2004, Lindstrom, with well-known industry leader Phillip Kotler, wrote a fascinating and insightful book, *BRAND Sense*, published by Simon & Schuster, New York.

OPPORTUNITIES FOR ADVERTISING AND SALES PROMOTION PROFESSIONALS

According to the major industry publication *Advertising Age*, some $150 billion was spent on advertising in 2006, representing 3.8 percent growth over revenues of 2005. Internet ads were up over 2005 by 17.3 percent, while local newspaper ads were down by 3.1 percent. Ad dollars spent in 2006 by media were reported as follows:

Magazines	$29.83 billion
Newspapers	29.80 billion
Network TV	27.16 billion
Spot TV	17.23 billion
Cable TV	16.75 billion
Radio	11.06 billion
Internet	9.76 billion
Syndicated TV	4.24 billion
Outdoor advertising	3.83 billion

Spending by advertising category was reported as follows:

Automotive	$19.80 billion
Retail	19.11 billion
Telecom	10.95 billion
Medicine/remedies	9.19 billion
General services	8.70 billion
Financial services	8.69 billion
Food/beverages/candy	7.23 billion
Personal care	5.73 billion
Airlines/hotels/car rentals	5.42 billion
Movies/video/music	5.38 billion
Other areas	48.49 billion

Although the types of ad campaigns, specific uses of media, and amounts spent on advertising may vary, companies will continue to use advertising to communicate with customers, and consumers will want to see ads that introduce new products. A slowdown in the economy suggests that fewer dollars will be spent on high-profile, expensive advertising campaigns in the immediate future. Less expensive avenues such as websites, newspapers and magazines, radio advertising, direct selling, and public relations may benefit from a recession economy.

B to B magazine reported that overall ad spending in 2006 reached $149.6 billion, up more than 4 percent from the year before, with the three agencies in the large agency category producing the highest revenues being McCann Erickson, Ogilvy North America, and BBDO New York. In the small agency category, the three top producers were Mobum Group, PJA Advertising and Marketing, and Stein Rogan and Partners. The top three in interactive media were Modem Media, OTOi, and Digitas.

Large advertising agencies offer clients comprehensive services, often including sophisticated marketing research and in-house production facilities. Smaller firms typically are willing to negotiate on commissions and are often more flexible in their approach to satisfying their clients' needs. Many of the top U.S. agencies are headquartered in New York City and maintain satellite offices around the world.

The growing African-American and Hispanic American/Latino markets form two huge consumer groups that have received much attention from the advertising world in recent years. Marketing research and polling firms frequently conduct surveys that measure the growth and importance of the Hispanic American/Latino market. African-American ad agencies have capitalized significantly on the multibillion-dollar urban market with an understanding of its culture and its appeal to all youths. Online advertising geared to the African-American community has also been growing fast.

In Canada, most major global ad agencies have offices in Toronto. In 2007, IAB Canada (Internet Advertising Bureau Canada) reported significant recent growth in Internet ad revenue, which broke the $1 billion mark for the first time in 2006. Moreover, about a 32 percent increase was expected in 2007. Online classified and directory sites, e-mail advertising, ads linked to search results, and online display advertising all showed substantial increases and were expected to do so again in 2007 and 2008.

Both the central government of Canada and the government of Quebec maintain promotion offices in the United States, with public relations and promotion specialists working to expand knowledge about Canada and Quebec by U.S. citizens, including cultural differences, and foster a good relationship between countries, as well as support the sale of Canadian products in the United States.

Advertising and sales promotion in Canada differ from practices in the United States in both magnitude and style. With Canada's population approximately 10 percent the size of the U.S. population, agency accounts are often considerably smaller. More specific government restrictions limit what can be said on broadcast media, both about products being offered and about their competitors. People seeking employment in Canada should be fluent in both English and French. A free booklet entitled "So You Want to Be in an Advertising Agency" can be obtained by writing to the Institute of Communication Agencies (formerly the Institute for Canadian Advertising) at 30 Soudan Avenue, Toronto, Ontario M4S 1V6, Canada, or you can go to the website, ica-ad.com, for more information.

In China, Internet ad revenues seem to be on the rise, although estimates of actual growth vary somewhat. Revenues are thought to be close to $1 billion for fiscal 2007, representing solid gains for most of China's major advertising companies. By comparison, *eMarketer* estimated in October 2007 that the U.S. market would exceed $21 billion in 2007 and would double by 2011.

EMPLOYMENT OUTLOOK

An average increase of about 12 percent in the number of jobs in the advertising and marketing management areas is projected between 2006 and 2016, which is about the average growth rate for all job categories. Jobs for advertising and promotion managers are expected to grow less, at about 6 percent, while jobs for managers of marketing are expected to grow more, at 14 percent, according to data from the National Employment Matrix, published by the U.S. Department of Labor. The actual number of management jobs is expected to grow by about 193,400, for a total of 1,833,000 employees in the marketing area, by 2016.

Although demand is strong for advertising and sales promotion executives, the new graduate enters a highly competitive job market. College preparation for entry-level jobs is oriented toward the development of job-specific attributes gained through courses in advertising, journalism, and business. Recruiters are looking for students with skills in advertising coupled with courses in areas such as history, humanities, and anthropology. Advertising graduates must be prepared to enter a competitive, global environment that will require a broader perspective.

Artists and multimedia designers accounted for about 218,000 jobs in the United States in 2006. Growth is expected to be at about 16 percent by 2016, a faster-than-average rate. Most of the jobs will be as graphic designers, animation artists, electronic media designers, and art directors.

The same growth rate of about 16 percent is expected for copywriters between 2006 and 2016.

Growth in the number of advertising salespeople is expected to be much higher than average over the next decade, with a 20 percent increase expected between 2006 and 2016.

It isn't unusual for advertising and sales promotion professionals to change jobs from corporate to agency settings and vice versa. Executive compensation levels in agencies are often tied to the size of the agency's billings, while corporate executive compensation varies with performance-tied bonuses. Entry-level salaries throughout the advertising industry are often low. The training and experience gained by beginners, however, enables them to more effectively compete for jobs higher up the ladder. Salaries increase considerably with advancement and are contingent on experience, job duties, and the size and prestige of the employer.

According to the U.S. Department of Labor's *Occupational Outlook Handbook*, 2007–2008 edition, salary rundowns for these professional groups are as follows:

Advertising Manager. About 38,000 jobs in this category existed in 2006. The median wage was $73,060, with employees in the lowest 10 percent earning $36,230 or less and the highest 10 percent earning $109,000 or more.

Advertising Sales Representative. Sales reps in the United States earn a wide breadth of salaries, wages, and commissions, with the median in 2006 being $42,750, the lowest 10 percent earning less than $21,460, and the highest 10 percent earning $91,250 and more. These jobs are expected to grow at a fast rate of about 20 percent through 2016.

Artist. Artists of various kinds held approximately 218,000 jobs in 2006, and the field is expected to grow by about 16 percent, which is faster than the average rate, through 2016. Most jobs are expected to be in graphic design, including electronic media, and in multimedia and animation. Median wages in 2006 were $51,350, with the lowest 10 percent at $30,390 or less and the highest 10 percent at $92,720 or more.

Copywriter/Copyeditor. This area also is expected to grow faster than average, at 16 percent, from 2006 to 2016. Median wages in 2006 were $46,990;

the lowest 10 percent received $27,340 or less, and the highest 10 percent received $87,400 or more.

In general, higher salaries were received in motion picture, multimedia, and electronic media; lower salaries were earned in print media positions for newspapers, books, and magazine publishing. In general, too, larger ad agencies paid more than smaller ones, and government jobs in general paid more than others.

ADDITIONAL SOURCES OF INFORMATION

Numerous books and periodicals about advertising and sales promotion are available. Of all career areas in marketing, these fields are covered in the most detail. In addition, trade associations offer a large amount of general information on the fields and professional development. The following is a partial list of resources.

Publications. Among the dozens of excellent periodicals for advertising professionals are *Advertising Age* and *Brandweek*, weekly publications found in most large public and college libraries. Both also maintain extensive and useful websites. *Marketing News*, the flagship publication of the American Marketing Association (AMA), is another rich source of information.

People interested in media can benefit from reading *Broadcast Week* and *Marketing and Media Decisions*. Job seekers can also consult directories such as *Roster and Organization*, published by the American Association of Advertising Agencies, and the *Standard Directory of Advertising Agencies*, to identify potential employers in the areas where they want to work and live.

On the Internet, visit webpronews.com and btob.com to learn more about agencies working with Internet advertising.

Associations. Some of the largest and most respected associations for advertising and sales promotion professionals are listed next. Some offer student memberships at a discounted rate, and almost all provide information that is especially useful for career planners and job seekers, including newsletters and other publications.

Advertising Club of New York
235 Park Ave. S., 6th Flr.
New York, NY 10003
theadvertisingclub.org

Advertising Council
815 Second Ave., 9th Flr.
New York, NY 10017
adcouncil.org

Advertising Research Foundation
432 Park Ave. S.
New York, NY 10016
arf.org

Advertising Women of New York
25 W. Forty-fifth St.
New York, NY 10036
awny.org

American Advertising Federation
1101 Vermont Ave. NW, Ste. 500
Washington, DC 20005
aaf.org

American Association of Advertising Agencies
405 Lexington Ave., 18th Flr.
New York, NY 10174
aaaa.org

Association of Promotion Marketing Agencies Worldwide
750 Summer St.
Stamford, CT 06901
apmaw.org

European Interactive Advertising Agency
6 Silkweavers Mews
Rothwell, Northants NN14 6FY
United Kingdom
eiaa.net

Interactive Advertising Bureau
116 E. Twenty-seventh St., 7th Flr.
New York, NY 10016
iab.net

Promotion Marketing Association of America
257 Park Ave. S., 11th Flr.
New York, NY 10010
pmalink.org

Radio Advertising Bureau
125 W. Fifty-fifth St., 21st Flr.
New York, NY 10019
rab.com

Retail Advertising and Marketing Association, International
325 Seventh St. NW
Washington, DC 20004
ramanrf.org

Television Bureau of Advertising
3 E. Fifty-fourth St.
New York, NY 10022
tvb.org

World Federation of Advertisers
120 Avenue Louise
1050 Brussels
Belgium
wfanet.org

Internships. The American Advertising Federation is an excellent source of advertising internships offered by many of its members. A membership list can be obtained by writing to the organization. You can then check the websites of the companies that interest you to see if they offer internships.

Internships in advertising are offered during summers, winter recesses, and regular school terms. Because internships are such a desirable way to break into the field, applicants face stiff competition. Applicants should develop a good resume, target an area of specialization in which they would like to work, and use all available resources to get leads on possible spots.

CHAPTER 5

CAREERS IN PUBLIC RELATIONS AND CUSTOMER SERVICE

The basic mission of public relations, or PR, is building, maintaining, and improving the public image of a prominent figure or organization. This responsibility may include writing press releases; lobbying; monitoring societal and environmental changes that may affect the subject's image or functions; communicating information both inside and outside the organization; and working with other specialists internally and externally in market research, advertising and promotion, product planning and development, finance, administration, and other areas to coordinate efforts and maximize the benefits to the organization of each special area of work.

During times of crisis control or special needs of any kind, the public relations specialist may work around the clock and be on call twenty-four hours of the day. For example, the public relations director for a supermarket chain that has had a problem with a food product or the public relations specialist for a political candidate in an election campaign can almost certainly plan on getting very little time off, and possibly very little sleep, for the duration of the endeavor. At other times, each may be able to quietly and systematically plan, organize, and create a public relations campaign in a more developmental fashion.

THE VALUE OF PUBLIC RELATIONS

Any smart businessperson knows that it costs a lot less to hold on to customers than to acquire new ones. Low prices and narrow profit margins, the high cost of implementing new technology, better-educated and more price-conscious consumers, and expensive advertising and sales promotion make good public relations and customer service all the more necessary to the success of a company. Building relationships is the way to keep customers loyal. Public relations provides the means of building a positive relationship with the community, while customer service fosters a long-term relationship with the individual customer.

SPIN, DAMAGE CONTROL, AND ETHICS

Public relations has the task of putting a positive spin on news that may seem to present the organization or individual in a negative light. Both the pharmaceutical firm that has been accused of being less than transparent in divulging information about side effects of a new product and the auto manufacturer that has had to recall a product are in urgent need of public relations professionals who can control the damage that such situations can cause to the company's reputation and sales. The public relations specialist has the challenge of remaining completely truthful while convincing the public of the ethical stand that the organization is making in addressing the situation. Because of the unethical practices of some organizations in the past, there is ongoing concern about honest presentation. Consumer and watchdog groups, through initiatives such as the Center for Media and Democracy's PR Watch, the free e-mail newsletter "The Weekly Spin," and the Center for Responsive Politics website, Opensecrets.org, maintain vigilant oversight of a broad spectrum of advertising, marketing, and public relations activities and are quick to point out problems.

In many other countries of the world, no such industry watchdog organizations exist. In fact, some countries have much different ideas of ethical business practice. The paying of bribes, for example, which Americans do not consider ethical, is routine in some countries and is accepted without objection. In a global marketplace, the public relations professional must quickly become knowledgeable about local customs in every area in which the client does business and must be prepared to deal with them with respect and diplomacy, while still maintaining all the ethical requirements of his or her own organization and country of origin.

THE ROLE OF PUBLIC RELATIONS IN SALES PROMOTION

Public relations involves the intentional creation of favorable publicity. Press releases are written so that they qualify as news.

Publicity is any information about the company and its products, or about the public figure, that appears in the mass media as news. Unlike paid advertising, publicity includes news that may originate from the company, from other sources, or from the media, and it is not always good news. As news, publicity is impossible to control, but it is published or broadcast free of charge.

Organizations today depend on goodwill not only from consumers who make up the markets for their products but also from the public at large. The actions of an organization in producing and marketing its products sometimes have a broad impact. Public relations professionals must therefore understand the attitudes and concerns of various groups such as government agencies, environmentalists, consumer advocates, stockholders, and residents of communities in which the company operates.

Lobbying for favorable legislation and against unfavorable legislation is one of PR's numerous activities. Monitoring legislative and societal changes that could affect future actions of the firm and advising management accordingly is another.

A positive public image helps to promote a company's products. Because of the national attention to worthwhile causes that has been intensifying ever since the 1990s, many companies are engaging in what is called "cause marketing." For example, they help to sponsor and publicize fund-raising events for causes such as shelters for homeless people, child care centers, AIDS prevention and cure, and breast cancer research.

THE NATURE OF PUBLIC RELATIONS WORK

Entry-level work as an assistant account executive in public relations includes acquiring information from a variety of sources and maintaining files, both of which are fundamental parts of the research process. With experience, PR professionals begin to write press releases, executives' speeches, and articles for both internal and external publications. Other duties include working with media contacts, planning special events, and making travel and entertainment arrangements for prominent people.

Promotion to the position of public relations account executive depends on the demonstrated ability to generate innovative ideas, work well with others, and communicate effectively with groups of employees, media representatives, and clients. Once promoted to account executive, the professional works independently and directly with clients, planning and executing appropriate public relations campaign strategies for each one.

Advancement to public relations account supervisor carries with it responsibility over major campaigns and the budgets for groups of accounts. The director of account services in a public relations firm, often an owner or partner, typically oversees campaigns and budgets and works to attract new clients.

Public relations, similar to advertising and sales promotion, is campaign oriented. When a campaign is launched, working overtime is often necessary. Meals with clients and frequent travel are sometimes on the agenda. Deadlines and pressures are implicit in this type of work. The satisfaction derived from creatively planning a campaign and witnessing its success is worth the irregular hours and extra demands for those with the temperament and disposition for PR work.

Public relations firms and professionals may specialize in any of a number of areas, including the following:

- **Consumer Affairs.** Field inquiries from customers, prepare educational materials, and address consumer safety and quality issues.
- **Government Relations.** Lobby for or against certain legislation, research and present information to the staff of government agencies, and recommend legislation useful to the company.
- **Investor Relations.** Serve as a liaison between the shareholders and the company, prepare reports, plan meetings, address shareholder inquiries, and encourage investment.
- **Employee Relations.** Coordinate communications between employees and management by producing in-house publications and arranging meetings, seminars, and conferences.

- **Community Relations.** Organize programs, activities, tours, classes, and publications for schools, civic groups, neighborhood associations, and interested individuals.
- **International Relations.** Research foreign customs, prepare information to be used in foreign countries, entertain foreign visitors, and introduce the company abroad.
- **Media Relations.** Write and place press releases, produce clips for television, organize press conferences, and arrange appearances of company executives.

The type and amount of public relations effort in any of these areas depend on the size and nature of the organization. A small staff working under the director of public relations usually does in-house PR. Larger firms may even have two PR departments—one for internal and one for external public relations.

In PR firms, the number of employees, their titles, and the division of work usually depend primarily on the size of the firm. As with advertising, good PR work begins with research to determine a client's goals and how best to accomplish those goals in light of the client's needs and competition. This is true whether the client is an individual, a commercial business, or a nonprofit organization. The areas of specialization just listed have many responsibilities and activities in common that typify public relations work: research, writing, media placement, public speaking, and event coordination.

EDUCATION AND PERSONAL REQUIREMENTS

Top-performing public relations professionals possess certain skills and attributes that are necessary for most of the career's responsibilities. They include high intelligence, business knowledge, problem-solving ability, sociability, persuasiveness, a sense of urgency, self-confidence, assertiveness, empathy, and stamina. Individuals who possess most of these traits and who have excellent oral and written communications skills are the best candidates for successfully entering the field of public relations. Qualified applicants hold degrees in a variety of areas, encompassing communications, business, and liberal arts. When available, specific programs in public relations are usually offered through college and university communications departments.

OPPORTUNITIES IN PUBLIC RELATIONS

Public relations professionals are hired by many types of organizations, including businesses, nonprofit groups, trade associations, government agencies, colleges, large advertising agencies with PR departments, and public relations agencies that serve a range of clients, as well as by individuals.

Public relations agencies range in size from a single practitioner to megacorporations with thousands of employees. During the past few decades of mergers and acquisitions, some public relations agencies have become almost unbelievably expansive. Among the largest are Edelman Public Relations (Chicago/New York), Publicis Groups SA (Paris), Omnicom Group, Inc. (New York), and WPP Group PLC (London).

A giant in the industry is WPP, based in the United Kingdom. Because of its global influence and power, it is profiled extensively by various Internet reference sources, which provide a detailed history and lists of the many companies that have been made a part of this industry behemoth. WPP's fast growth has occurred primarily through buyouts—sometimes friendly and sometimes not—of other advertising, promotion, and public relations agencies, many of them giants in their own right. WPP Group includes more than eighty companies, with such famous public relations names as Burson-Marsteller, Cohn & Wolfe, Hill and Knowlton, and Ogilvy Public Relations Worldwide. WPP has more than thirteen hundred offices in ninety-two countries and more than fifty-five thousand employees.

Most PR agencies are small, employing fewer than a dozen people. Agencies located in smaller cities offer attractive job opportunities, usually with an opportunity to learn a breadth of skills in close personal training relationships with veteran PR professionals.

In Canada, major agencies are located in the large population centers of Ontario, Quebec, and British Columbia. In general, because of the relatively smaller size of Canadian markets, both the scope of projects and the budgets will be smaller than in the United States. Because of the needs within Quebec and the rest of Canada, applicants who are fluent in both English and French are given preference.

Until the recession of 2008, demand for new recruits in Canada and the United States was so strong that entry-level salaries were being raised at a higher rate than executive salaries. In all economic conditions, salaries in public relations positions vary according to the size of the agency, experience, geography, industry, and area of specialization.

According to the U.S. Department of Labor's *Occupational Outlook Handbook*, 2007–2008, median annual earnings for public relations specialists were $47,350 in May 2006, with the lowest 10 percent earning less than $28,080 and the highest 10 percent earning more than $89,220.

Anyone interested in PR work should try to get some meaningful experience prior to college graduation. Work experience and knowledge in an area of specialization or a specific industry are especially helpful. Internships during college or as a first job after graduation provide an excellent way of gaining experience. Employers use interns' skills to screen candidates for potential entry-level hiring. Because of the importance of internships and the competitive nature of the job market, many colleges and universities require internships for graduation.

Job applicants should prepare a portfolio of PR projects on which they have worked. The college campus affords many opportunities for involvement in such projects, such as joining the staff of the school newspaper, radio station, or television station or becoming active in student programs. Working as a volunteer on political campaigns can also be excellent experience.

SOURCES OF PROFESSIONAL INFORMATION

The supply of internships in public relations is limited. If you are interested in an internship, it is wise to gather information and apply as early as possible. Many professional public relations associations sponsor internships and will provide information about these and other opportunities for beginners.

Associations such as those on the following list enable members to share professional information, network, take part in seminars and conferences to maintain professional awareness and education, and remain current on trends that impact their work and careers.

Canadian Public Relations Society, Inc.
4195 Dundas St. W., Ste. 4195
Toronto, ON M8X 1Y4
Canada
cprs.ca

Council of Public Relations Firms
317 Madison Ave., Ste. 2320
New York, NY 10017
prfirms.org

Institute for Public Relations
University of Florida
PO Box 118400
2096 Weimer Hall
Gainesville, FL 32611
instituteforpr.org

International Public Relations Association, U.S.
433 Plaza Real, Ste. 275
Boca Raton, FL 33432
ipranet.org
Makes an annual award for Best International Campaign.

International Public Relations Association
1 Dunley Hill Ct., Ranmore Common
Dorkey, Surrey RH5 6SX
United Kingdom
ipranet.org

National Black Public Relations Society
6565 Sunset Blvd., Ste. 301
Hollywood, CA 90028
nbprs.org

PR Watch
Center for Media and Democracy
520 University Ave., Ste. 227
Madison, WI 53703
prwatch.org

Public Affairs Council
2033 K St. NW, Ste. 700
Washington, DC 20006
pac.org

Public Relations Society of America
33 Maiden Ln., 11th Flr.
New York, NY 10038
prsa.org
Maintains an extensive job center.

Women Executives in Public Relations
PO Box 7657, FDR Station
New York, NY 10150
wepr.org

Public relations periodicals offer a wealth of material regarding current happenings in the field as well as advice to professionals. Job openings are also published in the classified sections of various publications such as *PR Reporter*, *PR Week*, *Public Relations Journal*, *Public Relations News*, *Public Relations Quarterly*, *Public Relations Review*, and *Publicist*. Most can be found in public or university libraries, and all maintain websites with extensive information and subscription instructions.

THE IMPORTANCE OF CUSTOMER SERVICE IN TODAY'S ECONOMY

Our economy is service oriented. Even in the selling of goods rather than services, courteous and helpful interactions with customers add value to the product and contribute significantly to customer satisfaction.

Today's marketing organizations of all sizes realize how important customer satisfaction is, since retaining customers is less costly than finding new ones. One Fortune 500 company reorganized its sales teams into "customer-focused teams," comprising specialists on order management, system configuration, and personnel, in addition to establishing customer care centers and global support centers to help its field personnel solve customers' problems.

Most companies are attempting to build long-term customer relationships. Satisfied car buyers, for instance, tend to buy the same brand over and over. This return business can add up to hundreds of thousands of dollars over a lifetime.

No one ever gets a second chance to make a first impression, and sales personnel are being retrained to think in terms of customer service that gives a favorable impression the very first time and continues that pattern. Providing the kind of useful information that helps customers make intelligent choices based on their individual needs and values is the current orientation to selling and keeping customers. In B2B marketing, suppliers are in effect entering partnerships with customers by helping them to improve processes, reduce costs, and deliver quality. Successful customers buy more products from their suppliers.

Global competition, changes in technology, and shifting customer demands place pressure on companies to retrain personnel in order to function effectively in a dynamic marketplace. Using the new technology and focusing more on solving customers' problems are two issues at the heart of this retraining.

To retain a customer base, companies must find out what their customers' needs are and how well they are being met and must design products and services accordingly. Another key is employee retention. Experienced employees understand what customers need, and satisfied employees help customers buy more.

Smart companies respond to customer complaints with a prompt personal reply, sometimes accompanied by coupons and free products. Customer complaints can be a valuable source of information for product development. Sincere responses to complaints and follow-up corrective action can generate positive word-of-mouth advertising.

Adding value to products and services by providing better customer service is a practical competitive strategy for every company. Ways to add value include learning a customer's business and suggesting methods to improve it, issuing a guarantee, offering a free service, and presenting customers with desirable and cost-effective options. Online Public Relations (online-pr.com) provides PR professionals with a breadth of useful information. It is maintained by James L. Horton, author of *Online Public Relations: A Handbook for Practitioners* (2001).

CUSTOMER SERVICE SALES

Customer service is everybody's job—sales personnel; support staff who handle orders and problems; distribution personnel; and managers who assess customer needs, plan products to satisfy them, and train and maintain satisfied employees.

The position of customer service representative exists in many companies. We speak to one to set up accounts for banking, cable television, or utilities. These representatives deliver the company's product or service to its customers in addition to providing information and answering questions. They are the troubleshooters who field complaints, expedite repairs and maintenance, and explain warranties. These positions require courtesy, helpfulness, competence, and product knowledge. In the past, customer service was considered an area that supported sales. In today's service-oriented economy, this rapidly growing field has been accurately renamed customer service sales.

Roughly 78 percent of all jobs in the United States are in service industries. Customer service sales personnel include call center employees, stockbrokers, travel agents, insurance agents, real estate agents, property appraisers, health club operators, and owners of beauty salons, day care centers, and housekeeping services—to mention only a few. All of these individuals are selling services.

Many positions require the use of computers and knowledge of industry-specific software. All require excellent communications and marketing skills. Think about the millions of customers who call banks every day for product information and financial help. Banks must use customer-focused technology in call centers, adapt Internet and e-commerce capabilities, and hire and train personnel who exhibit a customer service orientation.

Cooperative programs between businesses and communities are yielding qualified customer service professionals. For example, a training program in customer service for job seekers over age forty, called Operation ABLE (Association for Better Living and Education) of Michigan, was funded through a grant from Ameritech and the SBC Foundation. This program was designed to help mature workers acquire customer service skills while providing businesses with skilled employees in the office, retail, and service sectors.

Another cooperative arrangement involved 800 Support, a supplier of technical and customer support services, and Southwestern Oregon Community College, the state of Oregon, the Oregon Economic Development Department, the city of North Bend, and Coos County. A call center established by 800 Support in North Bend offered five hundred new technology and customer service jobs and was staffed with area residents whom the college trained, free of charge. In addition, state economic development offices provided funding assistance for equipment and leasehold improvements for the company.

Customer service representatives are included within three different Occupational Employment Statistics categories, so numbers of new jobs are hard to estimate, but all categories are projected to have faster-than-average growth from 2006 through 2016. According to PayScale's Internet Salary Center (payscale.com), wages in 2007 for customer service representatives ranged from approximately $10.27 an hour for entry-level workers to more than $14.47 an hour for workers having twenty or more years of experience, with average pay for all representatives at approximately $12.37 per hour. Supervisors and managers make substantially more.

TECHNOLOGY AND CUSTOMER SERVICE

Well-trained customer service representatives aided by new technology can solve customer service problems more rapidly and easily than ever before. Customers today can choose their shopping venues from among freestanding establishments, e-mail, Web pages, and mail-order call centers. Regardless of how orders are placed, businesses must provide customers with a consistent level of service. To do this, many have invested heavily in enterprise resource planning and customer relationship management systems to solve customer service problems and to target the clients who produce most of their business.

MarketSoft Corporation, for one, has been recognized for its eMarketing applications, developed to help B2B and B2C (business-to-consumer) companies create, fulfill, and measure demand to improve marketing impact and profits. Servicesoft Technologies, Inc., also at the forefront, developed Servicesoft eCenter to provide integrated solutions that address all customer service demands on the Web, including self-service, e-mail management, and live interaction.

Customer intelligent enterprise (CIE) is the technology that goes one step further than customer relationship management (CRM) systems. While emphasizing rapid communications and interaction with customers, CIE gives call center employees the responsibility of helping to solve customers' problems rather than just cataloging their complaints.

ADDITIONAL SOURCE OF INFORMATION

To learn more about customer service, contact the following organization:

International Customer Service Association
401 N. Michigan Ave.
Chicago, IL 60611
icasa.org

CHAPTER 6

CAREERS IN INDUSTRIAL, WHOLESALE, AND DIRECT SALES

A career in B2B and B2C sales can be both personally and financially rewarding. In the past, many people were unaware of the number and variety of career opportunities in selling and sales management, and many held negative perceptions of sales careers.

In the twenty-first century, however, the blending of the goals of sales and consulting has provided a fresh impetus for bright, positive, and energetic people to choose this career. The stereotype of an aggressive, pushy, in-your-face sales rep has been replaced by the model of a knowledgeable sales consultant role, in which the sales rep routinely gives valuable advice. Consumers know that they can benefit from the relationship with a reliable sales representative whose up-to-the-minute awareness of product and market needs is generously shared with clients.

Trustworthy sales reps have always provided this kind of service, and they have usually outshone their competition by this strategy in the long run, but for too long, "energy and aggression" were touted by some managers as the only sales skills needed.

It's good news for the industry, the sales reps, and the consumers that the technique of "take the money and run" is out—and the strategy of "be the best possible adviser to every one of your consumers" is in.

This chapter spotlights careers in sales for manufacturers, wholesalers, and direct marketers. Sales careers in stores and other retail establishments are outlined in Chapter 7.

Some business schools offer undergraduate courses in personal selling, but it has been debated whether courses in personal selling concentrate enough on key skills needed in the industrial marketplace.

A recent survey of practitioners and educators indicated that course work should place a stronger emphasis on communications, critical thinking, and reasoning skills. Techniques such as individual student projects and presentations, discussions of selling issues and business events, guest speakers, role-playing, and team projects are fundamental to teaching these skills. Industrial marketers are working to establish better relationships with business schools and are offering more internships. Through sales-related internships and participation in professional sales organizations, students can gain valuable experience and determine whether sales is a profession they would like to pursue.

A metamorphosis from the in-your-face salesperson to the "relationship manager" philosophy began in the 1990s. Though successful sales personnel require many of the same attributes as in former years, they now also require a few more, as well as a new orientation. Solving problems and satisfying customers in addition to generating sales volume are measures of success. Some companies have tied salary to customer satisfaction and eliminated commissions in favor of bonuses based on corporate profits. This sales approach requires additional training, knowledge, and teamwork over what was usually provided in the previous system of individual bonuses based solely on amount of sales.

Sales professionals perform a primary function in moving products into the marketplace. After production, manufacturers may opt for any or all of the available channels of distribution, by selling products directly to customers, to retailers, or to wholesale intermediaries.

Wholesaling is the link between the manufacturer and the retailer who sells to consumers. Using wholesalers is sometimes referred to as "two-step distribution." Wholesalers sell to retailers, other wholesalers, and manufacturers—almost everyone except the ultimate consumer. Although manufacturers can sell their merchandise directly to retailers if they wish, the wholesaling intermediaries provide many valuable services both to their suppliers (manufacturers) and to their customers (retailers). Often it is more cost effective for a manufacturer to sell goods at a reduced price through wholesalers, who then shoulder all the work and costs associated with sales personnel and warehousing.

Manufacturers that sell directly to retailers or to final consumers often tap the services of self-employed manufacturers' representatives. Well-known examples of this method include Avon and Mary Kay, both cosmetics and gift companies whose enormous independent sales-rep forces form the foundation of their success.

Direct marketing is in a growth trend again, largely due to consumers' increased interest in saving time and to the influence of the Internet. The term direct marketing refers to a variety of methods of nonstore selling, including direct selling, direct response retailing, database marketing, direct mail, telemarketing, and interactive marketing via the Internet. Both manufacturers and retailers use direct marketing.

THE SALES PROFESSIONAL

Regardless of employer or type of sales (industrial, wholesale, retail, or direct), sales professionals perform the same functions. Selling can be grueling work with long and irregular hours, extensive travel and entertaining, and sometimes reluctant and unwilling customers. Sales representatives must possess self-confidence, persistence, and optimism. Excellent communication skills are likewise essential, because sales representatives are also expected to be technical advisers, educators, and trainers. Part of the art of selling is persuading potential customers that a product will best solve their problems and satisfy their needs. People want clean carpets, not vacuum cleaners; peace of mind, not insurance; happy children, not toys. Therefore, to sell a vacuum cleaner, insurance, or any other product, a sales rep must persuade potential customers that this product is the best on the market to satisfy their needs.

The hard sell is definitely out of style. The effective salesperson today helps the customer to buy. This is done through first asking questions to better understand the customer's wants and needs and then providing information that helps clarify these needs. Then, while making recommendations, the sales rep talks about company products and their advantages to the customer. The emphasis remains on the customer.

Customer service is the concept behind successful selling, which requires individuals who are genuinely interested in their customers, want to see them happy with their choices, and can skillfully communicate this desire. Sales representatives are selling themselves and their companies, not merely their products, and honoring this precept is essential to building repeat business. They are gaining loyal customers, not merely making onetime sales.

THE NATURE OF SALES WORK

Sales representatives perform numerous activities, including these:

- Setting goals, planning, and scheduling
- Identifying and contacting prospective customers
- Maintaining contacts with current customers and anticipating their needs
- Planning and making sales presentations
- Reviewing sales orders, scheduling delivery dates, and handling details
- Maintaining up-to-date records and reports
- Addressing complaints and problems
- Monitoring the competition
- Learning new product information and marketing strategies
- Evaluating price trends and advising customers

Time management is crucial to successful selling. Sales representatives must carefully allocate their time among all of the foregoing activities. Some industries have cycles with peak selling periods, during which more time must be spent on customer contact. Slack periods provide time for record keeping, following up with customers, and researching new products. The steps of the selling process are as follows:

Step 1: Prospecting
Step 2: Preparing the preapproach
Step 3: Approaching the prospect
Step 4: Making the sales presentation
Step 5: Handling objections
Step 6: Closing the sale
Step 7: Following up

The computer is a sales rep's best friend. Today, almost all sales representatives must use state-of-the-art electronic technology to make their jobs easier, process data more quickly and accurately, and manage increasingly more detailed records.

Sales automation is a huge industry. Prices of laptops and notebooks are falling, making them more affordable. Personal computers and notebooks aid in record keeping and information gathering. Car and cellular telephones save time. Fax machines and communication networks get information to customers and the home office quickly. Generating and responding to leads is enhanced by such tools as broadcast voice mail that can leave dozens of personal messages per hour, predictive dialers that deliver a prerecorded message to thousands of consumers each day, and Internet technology providing access to customer demographics and credit information and the ability to respond to thousands of leads, track the results, and provide options for follow-up. Using technology is essential for sales professionals to compete successfully in the modern marketplace.

A college degree in marketing or an industry-related area is preferred for many positions in sales, but it is not always necessary for entry-level jobs. Promotions to company manager are, however, usually given to those with at least two- or four-year college degrees. The professional association Sales and Marketing Executives International (SMEI, www.smei.org) offers a certification program for sales and marketing managers. The SMEI Accreditation Institute verifies educational experience, knowledge, and standards of conduct pertaining to candidates for certification.

INDUSTRIAL SALES AND WHOLESALING

Computers and communications networks are having an enormous impact on the relationship between suppliers and buyers. Computer links between suppliers and targeted consumers are beginning to eliminate the need for some intermediaries. Database technology has helped retailers and wholesalers alike to determine exactly what products are needed and when. The stocking practices of both have become more efficient and less wasteful. In the computer industry itself, where items become obsolete quickly, products must be sold immediately.

Various opportunities and work environments exist in industrial sales and wholesaling. Sales representatives are employed by manufacturers or merchant wholesalers, or they can be self-employed as manufacturers' agents or wholesale dealers.

Company Sales Representatives and Managers. Sales representatives employed by companies are typically given training and expense accounts. Depending on the company's products, they may sell to wholesalers, to retailers, directly to industrial users, or to individuals through manufacturers' outlet stores. Inside sales reps, and sometimes customer service reps who also do sales, usually work in an office and solicit or take orders by phone. Some also work from home, often on a part-time basis. In addition, they process orders and monitor inventory. Field sales workers visit customers to solicit sales, provide information on new products, or render technical assistance. Some sales representatives also provide services to retailers, such as checking and reordering stock, and executing or suggesting promotion and display techniques. Industrial or electronic equipment sales representatives may install and service what they sell. Sales representatives also often work with purchasing agents and other buyers for customer companies.

Sales Management. Management structures vary. In large companies, sales representatives work under a district manager and, if promoted, may hold that position themselves. Levels of management within companies differ according to the organization's size and structure, but most sales representatives report to a sales manager.

The sales manager establishes training programs, assigns territories, and defines goals for the sales reps. The ability of sales managers to train and develop others is one key to their success and subsequent promotion. District sales managers may work under product or brand managers, depending on the company and its wares. Sales managers gather information from dealers and distributors on customer preferences. In addition, they project future sales and inventory requirements for the geographic area that they have been assigned. The district sales manager reports to the regional sales manager, who reports to the national (and perhaps the international) sales manager, who works directly with the vice president of marketing. Not all sales representatives aspire to climb the corporate ladder, and many prefer the autonomy of sales work to the headaches of management. It is not unusual for high-performing sales representatives on commission to earn more than their managers, whose salaries are fixed.

Purchasing Agents. Companies usually employ purchasing agents to obtain items and materials that they need for production. In smaller organizations, they may also handle purchases of goods and services that are needed for day-to-day operations. Purchasing agents also are employed by local, state, and federal governments as well as by the military services. Normally specializing in one product or group of products, they shop for the best quality at the lowest price. Purchasing agents arrange payment and delivery of products according to the employer's specifications. They may deal with company sales representatives, manufacturers' agents, or wholesale intermediaries.

As a field, purchasing is becoming more complex. People interested in purchasing as a career should study negotiation, purchasing law, international purchasing, federal regulations, international customs and duties, computerized purchasing, and product liability. College and graduate-level purchasing programs are including more training in international buying. Well-trained and highly experienced purchasing professionals are in increasing demand.

Manufacturers' Agents. Manufacturers' agents or representatives—called manufacturers' reps—are independent businesspeople who may sell one product, a group of similar products, or a variety of products to different types of customers. Usually they are assigned an "exclusive" territory in which only they can sell their company's line. The manufacturer pays the rep a commission for each sale.

Manufacturers' representatives are independent. They have no expense accounts or company benefits, unlike company-employed sales representatives. What they do have is total freedom—the advantage of being self-employed. Manufacturers' representatives are seasoned sellers, not beginners. The best preparation for obtaining permission—a formal agreement—from a company to sell its products is to first gain experience by working as a company-employed salesperson within the industry. When an experienced sales representative becomes a manufacturers' representative, he or she becomes an agent who provides an invaluable service to manufacturers who would not otherwise be able to afford such top sales representation. The manufacturer pays a commission only on products sold, and ambitious agents can earn sizable incomes if they are excellent salespeople.

Merchant Wholesalers. Approximately 80 percent of wholesaling establishments, accounting for slightly more than half of wholesale sales, are classified as merchant wholesalers. These independently owned businesses purchase products from the manufacturers and resell them to other manufacturers, wholesalers, or retailers. Usually referred to simply as wholesalers, those specializing in industrial products are often called industrial distributors, and those specializing in consumer products are called jobbers. Wholesalers may provide a range of services, including ordering, shipping, warehousing, and credit. They may stock a variety of products, one or two product lines, or, in the case of specialty wholesalers, a special part of a product line.

Wholesale Dealers. Basically, the job of wholesale dealers, also called merchandise brokers, is to bring buyers and sellers together. These dealers or brokers may work for either the buyer or the seller. Whoever employs them pays the commission. Typically, wholesale dealers will locate the products specified by their client companies at the best price, add their commission (usually about 30 percent), and give the customer the quote. Although the dealer may negotiate deals on behalf of the client, the client decides whether to accept or reject these deals.

If employed by manufacturers, the dealers will find a customer for the manufacturers' products and negotiate deals. These brokers or dealers handle both goods and services. Most familiar to individual consumers are the real estate, insurance, and investment brokers.

Other Wholesalers. Numerous other types of wholesalers provide similar wholesaling services, as well as career opportunities for people interested in wholesale sales. Included are petroleum bulk plants and terminals, which resell petroleum products to industrial users, retailers, and other wholesalers. Farm product assemblers buy grain, cotton, livestock, fruits, vegetables, and seafood from small producers to sell in large quantities to central markets or food processing companies. Public warehouses store bulk shipments and break them up for resale in smaller quantities. Resident buying offices offer a collection of merchandise, such as apparel, from various manufacturers for resale to small retailers who cannot afford to go to market frequently.

Trade Show Planning and Management. Industry trade associations and trade-show management organizations sponsor trade shows that enable producers, wholesalers, retailers, and customers to view and discuss their industry's product offerings. These shows vary in size and function and can require months, and sometime years, of organization.

Because of the increasing popularity of trade shows, their planning and management offer many new marketing career opportunities. In addition to the exposition or show manager, professionals from marketing research, advertising, sales promotion, and public relations are employed to make the trade show a commercial and professional success.

Show managers have a variety of responsibilities that include the following:

- Arranging lodging, meals, and transportation for exhibitors
- Overseeing preparation of exhibit directories, organizing display space and equipment, and hiring temporary personnel such as receptionists and clerks to work before and during the event
- Directing the marketing effort to attract exhibitors and attendees and provide them with information

Beyond job opportunities with industry trade associations and trade show management companies, exhibitors hire marketing specialists to determine shows in which to participate, to plan the exhibit, and to staff it with sales personnel. The individual exhibitors may also hire exhibit designers, who specialize in creating the most positive image for a company and its products, and contractors who work with the designers to build and prepare the exhibit booth.

E-COMMERCE AND ONLINE TECHNOLOGIES

Electronic commerce has experienced tremendous growth in recent years. One of the impacts of electronic commerce is to allow suppliers to more easily submit competitive bids for contracts with manufacturers. The complex relationships that big manufacturers develop with suppliers are likely to continue as before, but the use of online technology reduces some of the costs of doing business and improves efficiency.

A number of companies produce Web-based order-management tools that enable users to manage the timing of product offerings, order processing, generating order histories, tracking products, and other aspects of distribution. Online sites also enable customers to see parts and products, distributors to store large amounts of product information, and vendors to offer technical support. Other programs allow service providers to monitor sales leads, compute returns, and measure responses to their marketing and sales follow-up programs.

Although manufacturers are wary of upsetting the retailers who sell their products, the Internet cannot be ignored. It offers them an opportunity to showcase their products, establish direct links with consumers, and increase profits.

THE GROWTH OF DIRECT MARKETING

The phenomenal growth in direct marketing, or nonstore selling, is another testimony to the desire of the American public to shop quickly and easily. From the company standpoint, direct marketing lowers selling costs, because selling via mail, telephone, or computer is less expensive than in-person sales calls.

Mail-order shopping is nothing new to rural and small-town residents, and to many big-city people as well, who benefit from shopping from home. Early mail-order houses such as Sears and Montgomery Ward began with the expansion of the railroads and the postal service after the Civil War and developed into large businesses, providing rural shoppers with variety, convenience, and low prices. The "big books," or main catalogs, of the major mail-order houses such as Sears and Montgomery Ward were referred to as "wish books" by several generations of Americans. In the Broadway show *Finian's Rainbow*, a fast-paced production number called "The Great, Great, Come an' Get It Day!" lets the entire chorus parade the wonderful wishes that have come true in their fictional Southern town when their mail-order purchases arrive from the "Shears and Robust" catalog.

Today, a variety of proven methods can be used to reach shoppers in towns and cities of all sizes, including direct selling, direct response retailing, database marketing, direct mail, telemarketing, and e-marketing via the Internet.

The growth in direct marketing has created abundant career opportunities for professionals both in sales and in other areas of promotion such as advertising and sales promotion. Direct marketing is conducted by firms that sell products from other companies and by firms and individuals selling their own products. Every imaginable type of product is sold through direct marketing—apparel, housewares, cosmetics, toys and entertainment products, plants, computers, insurance, travel services, portraits, aluminum siding, pay-per-view television, even steamy love novels personalized with customers' names for the major characters. Ancillary marketing careers in direct mail selling include marketing researchers, product planners, catalog copywriters, designers, photographers, customer service representatives, and physical distribution specialists.

DIRECT SELLING

Direct (door-to-door) selling, also called direct retailing, is almost an American tradition. Many of us have sets of encyclopedias, hairbrushes and household products, and vacuum cleaners to prove it. In the comic strips, Dagwood Bumstead waged war for years on door-to-door peddlers who were both resourceful and determined.

Originally in Dagwood's day—the 1930s and '40s—door-to-door salespeople could literally walk door-to-door through a neighborhood and ask to be admitted to people's homes to show their wares and give their sales pitch. Modern-day door-to-door salespeople are up against many more local ordinances and different customs and customer expectations, and most must set up appointments with customers before making any home sales calls.

Direct selling is defined as the marketing of products directly to customers through personal explanation and demonstration in their homes or businesses. Direct sales representatives receive training in ingenious ways to sell a product, including some imaginative and engaging demonstrations. Avon, the largest cosmetics firm in the world, employs a huge number of door-to-door representatives. They work autonomously, setting their own timetables. Other well-known companies of this type include Amway Corporation and Mary Kay Cosmetics.

Although actual door-to-door selling is waning, party-plan selling, institutionalized by Tupperware, is still going strong. Party-plan salespersons recruit hosts to give parties at which they demonstrate and sell their products, sharing some of the profits and gifts with the venue provider.

Requirements for direct selling careers include a pleasant, outgoing personality and a lot of initiative. A high school education with some courses in speech and business is helpful. Although a college education is not required, courses in business, marketing, psychology, advertising, and sales promotion are useful. It is also necessary to know bookkeeping, accounting, local laws, and business license and tax requirements.

DIRECT RESPONSE RETAILING

Marketers advertise their products in magazines, in newspapers, on radio, on television, and through the Internet. In direct response retailing, also called direct response advertising, an address or phone number is given in the advertisement so that consumers can write or call to place an order. Credit cards and toll-free numbers have enhanced this type of marketing. Marketers often hire service bureaus to respond to calls and take orders.

Approximately twenty years ago, the home-shopping industry was born. Home Shopping Network and QVC Network sell such items as jewelry, home products, consumer electronics, apparel, sports gear, and toys to millions of viewers. Computerized voice-response call-handling systems are used to process calls efficiently and cost effectively. The home-shopping networks also use such marketing tools as celebrity endorsements and direct mail coupons.

DATABASE MARKETING

Database marketing is revolutionizing the way we perceive selling today. Sometimes called relationship marketing or one-on-one marketing, it involves the collection of massive amounts of detailed information on groups or individuals. Information collected from consumers over the Internet; from coupons, warranty cards, or sweepstakes; or at the time of purchase is combined with other data that is part of the public record, such as real estate transactions.

Sophisticated statistical techniques and high-powered computer technology are used to analyze and refine this input to identify specific consumer groups who share characteristics such as income, brand loyalties, and buying practices. These groups or individuals are then targeted as possible markets for new products, recipients of coupons, and entries to lists of potential customers that may be used, sold, or rented.

For example, companies and government agencies compile, sell, or rent lists of students, their schools, and their home addresses from kindergarten through graduate school. Based on demographic data such as income, number of people in the household, geographic location, home ownership, or college major, lists can be tailored for specific company needs. Sources such as birth and wedding announcements, magazine and catalog subscription lists, and professional membership directories are also used to create mailing lists.

One way to ensure being on numerous lists is to make a contribution or purchase via computer or mail; another is to be on a catalog subscription list. For example, consumers who purchase plants through the mail from one company are likely to receive catalogs or brochures soon from other companies that offer plants. The same is true for clothing or any other products.

TELESERVICES

Once used primarily as a marketing tool, telemarketing—or teleservices—has grown into a profession able to capitalize on developments in telephone technology and changes in the economy.

Marketing done over the telephone, called telemarketing or, more recently, teleservices, has experienced a marked increase since the 1970s, in spite of the recently enacted "Do-Not-Call-List" regulations. Abuses such as annoying selling techniques, too-frequent calls, and calls at the dinner hour were blamed for telemarketing's becoming a nuisance to consumers, and the Do-Not-Call regulations were the result. Although consumers can register their phone numbers on this national list, and the ability to opt out has had some effect on the industry, telemarketers continue to make significant sales and represent a large number of jobs, including a substantial number for part-time workers, students, senior citizens, and others who do not want to work full-time.

Some businesses have in-house telemarketing departments, but most use the services of telemarketing agencies organized much like advertising agencies and direct mail firms.

Teleservices is sometimes used in combination with direct mail or other advertising techniques. Inbound telemarketing involves receiving calls from prospective customers as a result of direct response retailing. These calls may be to place orders, seek information, or make complaints.

In outbound telemarketing, the marketer contacts prospective customers by phone to solicit sales. Telemarketers work from prepared scripts written to keep the consumer interested while encouraging purchase of the product or attempting to arrange a sales presentation.

Telemarketing may be done from a call center or a home phone, making it a convenient job for people with disabilities or for parents of small children. Phone companies and companies offering warranties on recently purchased products may use outbound telemarketing. Many firms use computerized phone systems that automatically dial a phone number and play a recorded message.

Telemarketing directors or call center managers oversee marketing operations, negotiate telephone contracts, and incorporate new telecommunications technologies into the marketing effort. Telesales representatives are trained on the job. A pleasant telephone voice and the ability to handle rejection graciously are required, since only a small percentage of all calls result in sales.

To alleviate a high turnover rate, this industry has developed career paths for its employees to include such positions as team leader, recruiting specialist, training specialist, and operations manager. These specialists hire, train, and motivate new personnel, prepare reports, make projections, and coordinate operations. Promotion to telemarketing director or call center manager usually requires several years of experience and a college degree in business, marketing, or a related area.

In addition to vacations and health plans, many teleservices firms offer other benefits such as 401(k) plans, individual or team bonuses, profit sharing, medical reimbursement plans, perfect-attendance awards, tuition reimbursement, and matching contributions for charitable giving. Salaries vary geographically and depend on whether the calls are consumer or B2B and whether they are outbound or inbound.

CATALOG RETAILING

Catalog retailing is popular among millions of loyal customers for whom it saves time, money, and travel. Among the thousands of companies that offer merchandise for sale through catalogs, the top catalog retailers include Lands' End, Lillian Vernon, and Hammacher-Schlemmer.

Growth in catalog sales peaked in the late 1970s and early 1980s. Although the rate has slowed, the catalog business is still growing. Catalog sales enable shoppers to select items from a vast array. Most catalog companies have liberal return policies. More and more products will be offered in new and innovative ways through catalog retailing. Though catalog retailing primarily employs order takers, there are also prominent positions for buyers, advertising professionals, and marketing managers.

DIRECT MAIL

Direct mail is one of the fastest-growing segments of the direct marketing industry. It includes catalogs sent by the Internet and through postal mail using promotional letters, coupons, and other materials touting products for purchase. Direct mail is used to produce leads, inquiries, orders, or an increase in store traffic. Another benefit of direct mail is that it enables producers to determine exactly who is buying their products. Advertising campaigns can then target identified markets.

Both specialized direct-mail firms and advertising agencies offer direct-mail services. In both cases, account services, research, creative, and media departments work together to develop the direct-mail campaign. The campaign focuses on established and potential customers. Companies may purchase targeted mailing lists from list brokers. List management firms—also called listing services—compile, sort, update, and rent lists of names. They employ list managers; sales personnel; computer personnel for data entry, programming, and analysis; and research personnel.

OPPORTUNITIES FOR SALES REPRESENTATIVES

According to the Occupational Employment Statistics survey for the U.S. Department of Labor, manufacturers and wholesale representatives held about two million jobs in 2006, with almost 60 percent of all representatives working in wholesale trades.

It is likely, considering the demographics of the American public and trends in lifestyles, that direct marketing will continue to grow at a faster rate than in-store marketing. Although fraudulent offers and questionable product claims cause consumers to be somewhat wary, items offered at reduced prices that can be ordered simply by dialing a toll-free number or clicking on an Internet icon hold definite attraction.

Earnings are difficult to project. Sales representatives may be paid on straight commission; thus, income is a percentage of sales made. It can fluctuate much depending on peak and trough selling periods within the industry and the economy, as well as on the ability of the salesperson. Sometimes sales personnel are paid a set salary plus a commission on sales. Some are paid a straight salary. Employers normally pay at least some commission as an incentive for sales representatives to generate more sales and thereby benefit directly from their efforts.

Employers offer numerous types of bonuses. The most common are given for meeting and exceeding sales quotas. Project-launch bonuses are customary in pharmaceutical and high-tech sales if a large percentage of the targeted accounts sign on. Bonuses can also be given for account penetration when sales are increased in underpenetrated accounts or product lines.

Manufacturers may offer sales personnel bonuses for increasing the participation of intermediaries, such as nonprofit or service organizations in product training, or for gaining information about competing businesses. Calling on personnel outside of purchasing who might influence a distributor's buying decision might likewise be awarded with a bonus. Many companies use bonuses as incentives. Insurance and real estate companies tend to favor contests and highly motivational prizes, such as trips, which may be used as an annual or semiannual sales incentives project.

Sales representatives must sell in order to earn their commissions. Employers usually offer beginners a salary or salary plus commission until they reach a predetermined sales level. Another common practice is to let beginners draw income against future commissions. If they are unable to generate sales, inevitably the sales representatives quit or get fired. Those who cannot sell cannot support themselves in a sales profession.

In big-ticket sales work, such as real estate, insurance, and financial services sales, annual income can be substantial, but statistics indicate that only the top 10 percent usually make a very large amount of money. For an individual who has the ability to be in this top-percentage group, there is no limit to income, and it can rival or exceed that of top management. For example, it is not unusual for large real estate companies to publish photos of their top salespeople along with announcements of their multimillion-dollar sales achievements.

According to the U.S. Department of Labor's *Occupational Outlook Handbook*, 2007–2008, median annual earnings of sales representatives in technical and scientific products were $64,440 in 2006. Most of these workers were employed in the following business categories: computer systems design and related services, wholesale electronic markets, professional and commercial equipment and supplies wholesalers, drugs and druggists, sundries wholesalers, and electrical and electronic goods wholesalers.

Wholesale and manufacturing sales representatives in nontechnical and nonscientific products made considerably less, with median earnings at $49,610. These areas encompass grocery and related wholesalers and non-durable goods wholesalers.

ADDITIONAL SOURCES OF INFORMATION

More information on careers in these parts of the sales industry can be obtained from the following professional associations:

American Teleservices Association
3815 River Crossing Pkwy., Ste. 20
Indianapolis, IN 46240
ataconnect.org

Direct Marketing Association
1120 Avenue of the Americas
New York, NY 10036
the-dma.org

Direct Selling Association
1666 K St. NW, Ste. 1100
Washington, DC 20006
dsa.org

Internet Marketing Association
10 Mar Del Rey
San Clemente, CA 92673
imanetwork.org

Manufacturers' Agents National Association
One Spectrum Pointe, Ste. 150
Lake Forest, CA 92630
manaonline.org

Manufacturers' Representatives
Educational Foundation
8329 Cole St.
Arvada, CO 80005
mrerf.org

CHAPTER 7

CAREERS IN RETAILING

The majority of people in the general population are most familiar with the sales and marketing roles related to retail sales. We all know salespeople in our own local grocery, supermarket, supercenter, pet shop, car dealer, jewelry store, bakery, tire dealer, gas station, candy store, bookstore, and computer supply establishments.

Most of us have been in and out of these retail sales outlets all of our lives, and we know a good salesclerk from a not-so-good one without thinking twice about it. We also know that these businesses are essential to the lives of our communities, and we are aware that they can be barometers of the overall economy—not only of the neighborhood but also of the nation and, now, even of the global community.

Retailing is a driver of the economy. Retailers must respond quickly to economic ups and downs and other factors that affect consumer shopping patterns, such as the increase in dual-income families, a higher birthrate, time pressures and other changes in lifestyle, increasing choices in products, and easier access to information. These factors have contributed to growth in the use of nonstore shopping, including home-shopping television networks, catalog retailers, and shopping on the Internet.

Today, retailers cannot direct all of their resources to in-store shoppers; they must figure out how to allocate these resources to selling opportunities outside the store to meet customer needs and maximize opportunities for both parties.

Generation Y, the population segment that embraces teens between the ages of twelve and nineteen, is estimated to grow to its largest number in U.S. history—thirty-five million—by 2010. Retailers are appealing to this vast market with special marketing designed to attract young people. A prime example is magazine-catalog hybrids called "magalogs," which link or blend products and stories and let customers have fun creating fantasy and adventure scenarios while buying products. Also in the mix are promotion campaigns that feature free CDs and music, contests, and more.

Another huge market has the attention of retailers: the seventy-eight million baby boomers, who make up 28 percent of the total U.S. adult population and represent $2.1 trillion in spending power. Those who are now aged fifty-five and older are quickly becoming the second most powerful demographic market in the country. Marketers are conferencing and planning for satisfying the wishes of these two groups as they change and acquire new lifestyles needs.

Among retailers that have become increasingly more family friendly are McDonald's and Starbucks, which have added play areas to many of their outlets; Home Depot, which has provided weekly workshops and other activities for kids; and Barnes & Noble, which added kids' menus and CD listening stations in some of its locations. L. L. Bean has created ten retail stores and plans to have thirty-two by 2012; its new program features an Outdoor Discovery School in which instructors give hands-on training in sports such as kayaking and fly-fishing. The company is also following the U.S. Green Building Council's LEED (Leadership in Energy and Environmental Design) standards for environmentally friendly buildings, using recycled materials and energy-efficient heating, lighting, and cooling systems.

Retailing is a combination of activities involved in selling goods and services directly to consumers for personal or household use. The activities of retail establishments include buying items from manufacturers and wholesalers, advertising, accounting, data processing, materials management, and personal selling, the latter being the key to successful retailing. Retail establishments come in all sizes, from large department stores to the tiny shop on the corner with one employee—the owner.

This chapter fleshes out in-store retailing. Chapter 6 addressed nonstore retailing. Retail professions fall into basically two groups: those involved in purchasing the goods offered for sale in retail stores, including merchandise managers, buyers, and assistant buyers; and those involved in selling goods to the public, including department managers and salespeople. This chapter explores these and other retail professions.

TRENDS IN RETAILING

Past spending by consumers, along with an uncertain economic outlook, rising energy prices, and other economic factors all affect retail sales. With a slowing U.S. economy, consumers have become more price conscious, and discount stores such as Target and Kohl's and online retailers have pulled some customers from the higher-end stores. Retailers that counted on a continuing economic boom and expanded too rapidly have been facing store closings and mergers since 2000, while all retailers have had to work hard to maintain their existing markets.

Many U.S. retailers have begun to expand their holdings into Canada in recent years. The number of Wal-Marts has increased; Home Depot has entered Canada; Gap and Price/Costco expanded their numbers of stores and Wal-Mart also expanded in Mexico.

The challenge to retailers in the future is to avoid high levels of debt, target specific markets, and use technology to reduce cost and improve service.

Price-conscious consumers are looking for bargains on the Internet and in establishments selling used merchandise, along with discount stores, warehouse clubs, and outlet malls. Recycling as a retail trend is evident in the growth of well-maintained used-merchandise stores that operate like any other retail establishment.

Specialty Stores

The specialty store rose to high levels of popularity during the 1980s, and this group has maintained most of its growth. This change in the shopping habits of the American public has been attributed to the needs of increasing numbers of working women. Such specialty stores as apparel stores, bookstores, toy stores, sporting goods stores, and others offer a narrow product line but a deep range within the line. They stock more styles, colors, sizes, or models with varying features, giving the shopper more choices. Shopping is less complicated and time consuming, because there are no long lines or confusing arrays of different departments.

Specialty stores are handy for lunch-hour shopping or quick stops after work. If a specific item is unavailable, shop owners are usually willing to order it and call the customer when it arrives. Many specialty shops open in strip shopping centers, because they are more convenient than large shopping malls. New businesses are covered more extensively in Chapter 10 under "Entrepreneurship."

Variety Stores

General merchandise stores such as department stores and variety stores have undergone some far-reaching changes over the years. Names such as Bloomingdale's, Macy's, May Company, Neiman-Marcus, Nordstrom, and Saks Fifth Avenue are synonymous with style. Although these stores have numerous departments, including toys, furniture, sporting goods, books, and home decorations, their real strength is clothing.

In order to compete with discount and specialty stores, department stores have introduced both budget shops and designer departments. For people engaged in fashion-related merchandising and sales, the greater emphasis on clothing is good news.

The 1950s through the 1970s saw the inroads of suburban shopping centers and the deterioration of downtown shopping. However, throughout the 1980s, downtown shopping malls began to develop again. Some of these malls contain fashionable department stores, specialty shops, and restaurants that cater to tourists, conventioneers, and lunch-hour shoppers in the downtown area. River walks and parkway and boulevard developments have been constructed to make these areas attractive and to draw customers to the area and keep them there.

Retailers must constantly adapt to changes in consumer shopping patterns. Walgreens, for example, started to sell bread, milk, butter, eggs, snacks, beer, wine, soda, and frozen TV dinners along with its usual drugstore merchandise. Though prescription and nonprescription drugs remain the fastest-growing portion of Walgreens' business and are likely to remain so as the population ages, this convenience-store approach to sales and marketing has worked well.

Discount Stores, Supercenters, and Warehouse Clubs

Mass merchandising retailers offer a variety of products usually at discount prices in large, self-service stores. Opportunities in sales are substantially reduced, purchasing is centralized, and services are nearly nonexistent. However, management opportunities exist in these stores, and many chains have experienced phenomenal growth. Discount stores, superstores, warehouse clubs, and warehouse and catalog showrooms are examples of mass merchandising retailers.

Factory outlet malls increased in number through the 1990s. Initially these outlet malls housed only manufacturers' shops, and some contained only upscale manufacturers. Now outlet malls are renting space to discount houses as well. Though the trend toward factory outlet shops and discount malls is likely to continue, newly constructed shopping malls have not all fared well since the recession of 2001, and many large spaces have remained empty.

Wal-Mart, needing new avenues of growth, acquired Wholesale Club, Pace, and Sam's to increase its share of the warehouse club business and now commands a large percentage of the warehouse club market.

Specialty retailers such as Home Depot, Office Depot, and PetSmart have imitated the format of the large variety wholesale clubs.

Following the recession of 2001 and the effects of the war in Iraq, retail sales continued to lag, and managers and salespeople strove to promote more business. The decline was attributed to several factors: the widening gap between rich and poor, reductions in the manufacturing segment of the economy, pressure from investors for higher profit margins, fewer available jobs in unskilled and semiskilled markets, and stiffer educational requirements for better-paying jobs.

Because of this shift, retailers have begun to cater more to low-income shoppers. The future looks promising for discount stores, supercenters, and warehouse clubs.

APPLYING ADVANCED TECHNOLOGY AND E-COMMERCE

Most retailers today place heavy emphasis on technology and professional management. For years, supermarkets and large discount stores have used computerized cash registers and point-of-sale terminals, which gather and process enormous amounts of consumer buying data. Up-to-the-minute sales information is available to more and more retailers. Executives with both merchandising and management skills who can increase profits and worker productivity through use of the new technology will continue to be in demand.

Large discount retailers exact careful control over their inventories by tying into their suppliers electronically. Electronic intercompany inventory management enables retailers and their suppliers to maintain inventory tightly, as needed, and has radically changed the ways that buyers work.

The National Retail Federation/Forrester Online Retail Index provides information to retailers compiled from monthly surveys of online shoppers detailing how much money is spent online and on what products. In a separate survey in 2006, results showed that Americans who use the Internet command 66 percent of the buying power of the total U.S. population.

The 2007 holiday buying period revealed new favorites, and Amazon .com cited Nokia Internet Tablet PC and Wii games as the top-selling items.

In the United Kingdom, Forrester Research reported twenty-seven million e-shoppers over the 2007 holiday season, which was a 42 percent increase from 2006. An estimated 61 percent of U.K. homes were online, amounting to more than fifteen million households, according to the National Office of Statistics. Nielsen/NetRatings indicated that the U.K. Internet population was well balanced between the sexes, with females at 48.5 percent and males at 51.5 percent.

Many unique challenges exist for both new Internet retailers and established retailers trying to maintain their market shares by tapping into the online bonanza. Numerous online companies have gone under with the slowdown of the economy. Funding dried up, consumers weren't buying, and some of the newest and most eager entrepreneurs realized that they needed to know a lot more about business.

Online shoppers still express concerns about shipping charges, the inability to judge the quality and fit of clothing items before purchase, return policies, credit card safety, delivery times, and the inability to ask questions about products. Nevertheless, the ongoing growth in Internet purchases suggests that convenience, time saving, and technology have a distinct appeal in today's culture.

RETAIL SALES

Customer service is the key to successful retail sales. A recent American Express survey revealed some differences in how customers of different ages value service, finding that the majority of shoppers over age fifty-five prefer personal attention from salespeople, those between thirty-five and fifty-five favor an easy return/exchange program, and shoppers under thirty-five are partial to fast checkout service.

Successful retail salespeople understand the preferences of different customers, know their store's merchandise, and are skilled in interacting with the public. Customers may come into retail establishments to purchase specific items, to comparison shop, or merely to browse. The people who deal directly with these customers can make or break a business. Three prerequisites for success in selling any product are the following:

- Ability to communicate well
- Courteous manner
- Positive attitude

Many people reject the idea of a career in sales because they dislike the hard sell. It also repels customers. The successful salesperson instead finds out what the customer wants and needs, determines what merchandise meets this profile, persuades the customer to buy it, and makes the customer feel good about the purchase. Essentially, the best selling is always helping customers to buy what they really need and want, and to buy it at a good price. Real customer service is the lifeblood of successful selling.

Mass Merchandising. The most basic type of sales and customer service occurs in mass merchandising, where customer inquiries usually have to do with whether the store stocks an item and where it is located. Knowledge of store layout and merchandise is necessary. Although these positions do not involve commissions and do involve stocking shelves more than actual selling, they provide reliable full-time and part-time jobs for people with little formal education and for students. They also offer experience that other employers often seek and can lead to supervisory positions in sales.

Specialty Sales. Sales work in fashion apparel, cosmetics, and numerous other product lines requires more in-depth product knowledge and sometimes requires special skills. For example, cosmetics salespeople sometimes give demonstrations as part of their sales presentation. Whether employed in a department of a large store or in a small specialty shop, good salespeople demonstrate friendly interest in their customers, a willingness to help, and considerable diplomacy. Some clothes do not look good on some figures; rather than selling a customer something that isn't flattering (a realization that the customer will reach sooner or later), a good salesperson will tactfully show the customer something that looks better. Helping customers requires much more than ringing up sales.

Commission Sales. In selling expensive products such as cars, computers, and appliances, salespeople must know and be able to articulate not only the capabilities of their products but also why their products are superior to those of the competitors. Therefore, they need to be familiar with the competing products. Salespeople working on commission can reap a large income if they generate many sales.

The Retail Sales Professional

To be successful, sales professionals should be able to do all of the following:

- Recognize the wants and needs of customers
- Become familiar with the market and the competition
- Understand and describe product features and uses
- Explain product benefits to customers
- Master effective selling techniques
- Realize the importance of customer service
- Maintain a positive attitude toward work

Although customers come to the store, a salesperson needs both initiative and a customer service orientation to close as many sales as possible. Too often in large department stores, the customer must seek out the salesperson. The salesperson with the initiative to approach the customer is far more likely to make the sale.

In retailing, it is imperative to understand the customer. For example, Brooks Brothers has catered to generations of men desiring traditional men's tailoring. When Marks & Spencer acquired Brooks Brothers, it dismayed many loyal customers by installing escalators in stores in 1989 and putting shirts and sweaters on open tables rather than in glass cases. These "innovations" along with jazzy new ads to attract a younger clientele brought a host of complaints from regular customers.

Every successful retail establishment has a solid customer base. Understanding the likes and dislikes of the store's traditional customers and keeping them happy, while also luring new customers into the store, is a strategic necessity for sales personnel and management.

Whether selling goods or services, the selling professional must be reliable and responsive. The customer may not always be easy to please. Selling requires self-control and diplomacy. Everyone does not have the temperament for selling to the public, but for those who do, sales can be a lucrative and rewarding profession. Although the majority of job opportunities within retailing are sales positions, there are other career options for individuals from a variety of educational backgrounds.

SALES MANAGEMENT

Sales management trainees may be recruited from the sales staff or from the pool of recent college graduates. Having an M.B.A. may not represent much of an advantage in the hiring process for beginning retail management positions, but it may qualify the applicant for a slightly higher salary, and of course, eventually, the knowledge and discipline of the M.B.A. will stand any businessperson in good stead.

In retailing, however, hands-on experience is essential. Compared with other marketing careers, experience is fairly easy for an applicant to obtain by working in a part-time retail sales position while in college. Though often minimum-wage jobs, these part-time positions can provide necessary experience to land a good job after graduation. Large department stores actively recruit on college campuses, providing an excellent way for prospective graduates to make an initial contact. Applicants should ask about each company's management training program, which most large companies offer and which are usually worthwhile in many respects.

Generally, beginning as a department manager trainee, novices work with experienced managers throughout the store to observe all aspects of store operations. Under supervision, trainees handle staff scheduling, customer complaints, and record keeping. Once a trainee has demonstrated the ability to supervise staff, work well with customers, and make good, quick decisions balancing the welfare of the store and the customer, the individual is promoted to manager of a small department.

The next level of promotion is usually to a larger department where the manager supervises more staff, oversees more merchandise, and manages a heftier budget. Such duties as scheduling workers, handling customer service requests and complaints, and monitoring how well merchandise is selling are all in a day's work.

Sales staff development is also important because, when promoted, department managers have already trained their replacements. Retail sales managers are usually given broad goals containing sales and profit expectations. How to reach or exceed these goals is up to the manager. Managers of exceptionally profitable departments are likely to be promoted to group sales manager. Experience in directing several department managers and coordinating a sizable portion of store operations may qualify an individual for assistant store manager, and then store manager. The best retail store managers are selected for top corporate positions. Upwardly mobile managers are often targeted early in their careers, and in large chains, they may be required to relocate every few years.

MERCHANDISE BUYING AND MANAGEMENT

Merchandising is a crucial part of the retail trade. Buyers purchase the merchandise that the store will sell. They decide what products will be offered for sale, arrange purchases from manufacturers, and set retail prices. Decisions are based on knowledge of customer tastes, changing trends, and a balance of quality and affordability.

To acquire the knowledge for making these decisions, buyers study marketing research reports, industry and trade publications, and detailed analyses of factors that affect the direction of the economy.

For example, it is speculated that clothing sales in many high-end stores did not grow as anticipated in the last few years because the largest segment of customers wanted more casual clothes instead of the elegant and tailored designer fashions that traditionally were the stores' particular strength.

Merchandise buyers were reluctant either to believe that the trend was real or to make the switch from their staple styles. As a result, increased markdowns of slow-selling items plagued the stores for several years.

Just a quick glance at the websites and catalogs of these same stores today will show that the new "wild-child" fashion finally won out—at least for a while. Buyers studied the market and its changing mood and began to acquire the styles that their customers really wanted. Gone were the grand old names and perfectly tailored suits and gowns, the fine fabrics, and the exquisite workmanship.

The customers—newer and younger—wanted short, gauzy tops layered above spindle legs, and a skimp of a scarf in spidery lace or sculptured velvet looped ever-so-carelessly around the torso, just above thin puce stockings and thinner-fabric boots.

Many of the buyers—especially the older ones—suffered at first: how were their customers going to clean those flimsy little garments without destroying them? Not our problem, said the younger buyers—it's what they want!

"Business casual" had fallen upon the workplace, and even the styles for social and cultural events such as theater, restaurant dining, and family celebrations had become much more casual as well. No one went about anymore in the old top-of-the-line fashions. And the buyers bowed to the new fashion. They knew that in fashion merchandising, it is a matter of commercial life or death to be constantly alert and ready to respond to the groundswell of a popular trend.

Because of the responsibility inherent in spending large amounts of the store's money, the training period for buyers can range from two to five years. The entry-level merchandising position for college graduates is assistant buyer. After some store training, usually in sales, an assistant buyer works under a merchandising supervisor. Duties usually include communicating with manufacturers and placing approved orders, inspecting new merchandise, and supervising distribution of the merchandise throughout the department. During the first two to five years in buying, the novice becomes acquainted with manufacturers' lines, the store's needs, and the competition and begins to recommend products for purchase. With promotion to buyer, duties expand to analyzing customer needs and choosing products to meet them. The role of the buyer underpins the success of any retail establishment. The Gap, for example, decided to decrease its in-store basics, denim and T-shirts, and add new items such as flowing skirts, embroidered tops, and accessories. Reducing the percentage of basic items puts more pressure on the buyer to choose the right merchandise mix.

Buyers normally begin in small departments and are promoted to larger departments. The most promising buyers become merchandise managers, whose primary duties are to supervise buyers. They oversee the department's budget, deciding how money should be divided among the buyers. Merchandise managers have a meaningful impact on their store's image, its product offerings, and the direction of styles. They must formulate a mix of brands to generate the most sales and profits, taking care to keep store brands from overwhelming others.

Distribution managers oversee the movement of merchandise. They are responsible for receipt, ticketing, storage, and distribution of a store's inventory. The growing problem of customer and employee theft has resulted in a new management position—loss-prevention manager, whose duties include tracking inventory, price overrides, refunds, and employee purchases. Point-of-sale and electronic article surveillance systems are also used for security in theft-plagued retail outlets. Buyers who have been promoted through various management levels often reach the position of corporate merchandise manager. In this position, they may approve buying decisions for several stores in a state or in an entire region.

The bread and butter of large department stores is apparel. To fill the specialized position of fashion coordinator, an individual needs a background in fashion design, a portfolio to show artistic talent, a keen sense of style, good taste, and an awareness of sound business practice. Some large department stores employ fashion coordinators to work with buyers in selecting merchandise. Although glamorous work, in that it may involve overseas buying, the position of fashion coordinator is not a line position leading to promotions into higher management. It does, however, afford people with backgrounds in art or fashion merchandising an exciting and satisfying outlet for their artistic talents.

Another position requiring an art background is display designer. Large retailers design window and interior displays to promote sales. Recent graduates begin as apprentices and are trained on the job. Competition is stiff for positions in fashion coordination and display, as opportunities are limited.

OPPORTUNITIES IN RETAILING

A tight labor market and a high turnover rate in sales positions put ongoing pressure on retailers to find workers for entry-level sales positions. In Chicago, the Retail and Education Alliance for Development of Youth (READY) program helps fill this need by training hundreds of high school students for subsequent placement in summer retailing jobs. Monster.com, the leading online careers site, links retail professionals with thousands of job postings. Just go to Monster.com and search under keywords *Retail Sales* for thousands of U.S. job listings.

Retailing will continue to employ large numbers of sales representatives. According to *Occupational Employment Statistics* survey data, there will be average growth in the numbers of jobs for retail salespersons, about 12 percent a year between 2006 and 2016. Median earnings were reported as $9.50 per hour in the OES report of May 2006. In a job area marked by plenty of turnover, the number of jobs expected is encouraging.

Wholesale and retail buyers earned median annual incomes of $44,640 in May 2006, but little or no growth is expected in the number of jobs in this area between 2006 and 2016. Buyers for farm products earned slightly more in May 2006.

ADDITIONAL SOURCES OF INFORMATION

Staying current on trends is essential to retail professionals, especially for buyers and for merchandise and department managers. Such periodicals as *Advertising Age*, *Chain Store Age Executive*, *Discount Store News*, *The Fashion Newsletter*, *Inside Retailing Newsletter*, *Journal of Retailing*, *Peterson's Job Opportunities for Business and Liberal Arts Graduates*, *Stores*, and *Women's Wear Daily* are available in most public and college libraries for people interested in retail careers. Directories of retailers, including *Fairchild's Financial Manual of Retail Stores*, *Nationwide Directory—Mass Market Merchandisers*, and *Sheldon's Retail Directory of the U.S. and Canada* can be found in the reference section of most city and university libraries.

As in other fields, retailing associations are another valuable source of inside information, such as those that follow:

American Marketing Association (AMA)
311 S. Wacker Dr., Ste. 5800
Chicago, IL 60606
marketingpower.com

International Mass Retailing Association
1901 Pennsylvania Ave. NW
Washington, DC 20006
imra.org

Mexican American Grocers Association
405 N. San Fernando Rd.
Los Angeles, CA 90031
maga.org

National Retail Federation
Liberty Place
325 Seventh St. NW, Ste. 1100
Washington, DC 20004
nrf.com

National Retail Grocers Association
1825 Samuel Morse Dr.
Reston, VA 22090
nrga.org

Sales and Marketing Executives International
458 Statler Office Tower #977
Cleveland, OH 44115
smei.org

CAREERS IN MARKETING MANAGEMENT

Managerial areas in marketing include advertising, marketing, promotions, public relations, and sales management, all of which relate directly to the success of the entire organization. These managers plan, carry out, and/or oversee the company's market research, long-range planning, marketing strategy, product planning and development, public relations, advertising, promotion, sales, and sometimes also the product scheduling and physical distribution.

Promotion to a top corporate marketing position may occur from within the company, or a manager may be brought in from outside. Throughout all the functional areas of corporate marketing, outstanding individuals advance to management levels. In a large corporation, the top position is executive vice president of marketing, the manager who has authority over all marketing activities of the business. Because of the breadth of the person's company knowledge and experience, often a marketing vice president will eventually advance to the position of chief executive officer.

The economic pressures of the last three decades have spurred corporations to streamline management structures considerably. In the 1970s, it was customary to have as many as twelve to fifteen levels of supervision in large corporations. These days, the norm is five or six levels. This change is the result of major restructuring brought about by a wave of acquisitions and divestitures, increased global competition, an attempt at creating a more entrepreneurial environment to foster development of new products, and fluctuations in the economy. The reduction of mid-level managers has increased both the complexity and the pressures of management positions.

THE RESTRUCTURING OF CORPORATE MANAGEMENT

The past three decades have been characterized in business worldwide by thousands of corporate mergers, acquisitions, and divestitures. As companies and pieces of companies were bought and sold, hundreds of thousands of managers and professionals were forced to change jobs or retire early. In many cases, mid-level management positions were never refilled. Major reorganizations took place in companies. Top management realized that if the company was to compete in a more competitive, rapidly changing business environment, it had to respond faster to change. Improved productivity and a leaner corporate structure enabled managers to introduce products into the market more efficiently.

For years, small companies have received the most credit for introducing new technology into the marketplace. One of the reasons for this accomplishment is the efficiency of a less formal corporate structure. In large companies, various levels of management extensively review plans for new-product development; small companies, functioning as entrepreneurial teams, are able to move a product rapidly from the drawing board to the marketplace. The message was clear: until large corporations became more entrepreneurial both in philosophy and in practice, they would be unable to beat their small competitors into the marketplace with new products.

Big companies responded to the challenge by creating more project or product development teams. These teams were given the authority to operate fairly autonomously both in fulfilling goals and in competing for company resources, as described in Chapter 3. Product managers reported directly to marketing managers at top levels in the company. Because the teams were entrepreneurial in spirit, yet part of a large corporation, the term *intrepreneuring* was coined.

With fewer levels of management and tighter budgets, companies were unable to reward managers with promotions and raises as they once had. However, fewer job titles and pay grades make it easier to base raises on performance rather than seniority.

One way that companies motivate promising new or upcoming managers is with a lateral or sideways move that offers a new challenge and the ability to learn other parts of the company's operations firsthand. Giving more responsibility and autonomy to subordinates is another way to keep them from getting bored.

Overseas assignments for managers are inevitable as companies expand their global operations. At companies in which a large percentage of sales are foreign, an overseas assignment is necessary for promotion to top management. Finally, more companies are offering up-and-coming executives mid-career breaks by sending them to management development programs designed by business schools especially for executives.

MARKETING MANAGERS

Top-level executives determine an organization's mission and make policy. The executive vice president for marketing directs overall marketing policy, the effect of which is felt at every level and function of the marketing process. The marketing management concept guiding the field today has broadened in scope because of the increasingly complex business and economic environment in which firms must operate.

The top marketing executive spends considerable time in analysis of research, using and executing econometric and other forecasts, creating detailed marketing plans, and presenting these plans to the CEO and other top officers. Top-level production and finance managers must be convinced that marketing policies will enable the company to meet its overall goals and objectives.

All marketing managers engage in planning, implementing, and controlling their organizations' marketing activities and decisions. These functions are common to all managers, but marketing managers at the top of the organization are primarily involved in planning. Planning includes setting objectives and standards of performance and developing strategies and tactics to implement those objectives. Marketing strategy addresses such issues as what markets to enter, what products to offer, how to allocate marketing resources, and, for many large corporations, what companies to buy. Marketing executives must make such global decisions in consultation with finance, production, and sales executives. When a project has been given management approval, objectives and strategies are communicated to lower-level marketing managers, who will immediately develop the more detailed marketing strategy required to implement the plans.

MIDDLE MANAGERS AND SUPERVISORS

Implementation involves organizing, staffing, directing, and coordinating the company's resources. All marketing managers are involved in implementation activities to some extent, but unlike top managers, who spend most of their time in strategic planning, middle-level managers such as department heads and project team leaders are primarily involved in implementation. Hiring staff, assigning duties, directing and overseeing projects, distributing the budget throughout the department, and other such activities are the responsibility of department heads.

Mid-level managers and supervisors are responsible for measuring staff performance to see that objectives are met and taking corrective action if they are not. Specific objectives related to deadlines for projects, planned budgets, and sales quotas are measurable. If objectives are not met, it is up to managers to determine whether they were unrealistic or whether either external factors or worker performance is responsible. Corrective action may take the form of revising objectives, making adjustments to allow for external factors, or working with staff to solve problems.

The work of middle managers and supervisors has been discussed throughout this book. They manage staffs of professionals and technicians working in the various activities of marketing. Managers of marketing research, product development, advertising, sales promotion, public relations, and regional sales all report to top-level marketing managers. In the absence of many levels of middle managers, these managers operate their departments more autonomously and have more authority over both activities and budgets. Their offices are usually located close to top management, and communications are considerably less formal than in the huge bureaucracies of the past. Though chain of command is still intact in many businesses where managers at every level formally report to a designated individual, communications are considerably more relaxed and pragmatic in most organizations.

The information technology revolution has brought sweeping changes that have transformed corporate communications forever. Each manager has a personal computer, which is usually hooked into a central computer through the company's local area network (LAN). Branch computers are hooked into the central computer through wide area network (WAN) technology. This improved communications technology has enabled the immediate and free flow of information throughout the organization. Management information systems and decision support systems disseminate information needed for management decisions.

A system is a collection of people, machines, programs, and/or procedures that is coordinated and organized to perform a certain task. Marketing information systems provide marketing managers with a steady flow of timely, accurate information from a variety of sources both inside and outside the organization that they can then use to make decisions. Computers and communications technology have reduced the need for some levels of managers whose main job was organizing and communicating this type of information.

SUCCEEDING IN MANAGEMENT

A top-level manager's background doesn't necessarily assure success within a specific corporate setting. Personality, character, and work style, as well as experience, education, and intelligence, all factor in the equation. For this reason, many companies, such as Bristol-Myers Squibb, Dell Computer, General Electric, and Motorola, have used psychological evaluations costing several thousand dollars apiece to help determine whether executive candidates will fit well into their corporate cultures. Multilevel interviews, meetings, and conferences with other members of top management will be involved, supported by communication with former colleagues, and careful review of achievements and details of work history are all taken into account.

Despite an individual's qualifications and talent, succeeding within a unique culture often depends on specific values and personality traits. Marketing professionals should carefully choose a company, find a mentor, and tap whatever resources are available. Choosing and being chosen by the right company is a complicated undertaking. Company offers to new college graduates may be evaluated in terms of salary, benefits, and growth potential.

Chapters 11 and 12 further plumb many issues that can help graduates evaluate the job market and the offers that they will receive. Little of the internal working of the company can be gleaned from company literature or job interviews. Only when working for a company can an individual learn the intricacies of how decisions are made and where power actually resides.

ATTRACTING A MENTOR

A mentor is an experienced professional in the same field, preferably one who has made steady career progress within the organization. Good mentors provide insight into the organization's culture, introductions to people higher up, and wise suggestions regarding the unspoken rules of the company. Every company has a unique corporate culture and its own way of doing things.

Finding a mentor is not easy. Any mentor worth having is usually extremely busy and is not out looking for protégés. The young employee who shows persistence yet flexibility, works hard to obtain recognition, listens to everything going on in the company before taking strong positions or forming alliances, has clearly stated career goals, and displays confidence and pride, as well as ability, will attract attention before long. Many employees have followed their mentors right up the hierarchy by filling the positions the mentors vacate on the way up.

WOMEN IN MANAGEMENT

In 2006, a record number of women were part of the U.S. labor force; at sixty-seven million, they represented nearly 46 percent of the workforce. Of those, 38 percent were in management, professional, and related occupations, according to the U.S. Department of Labor. More than 51 percent of all managerial, professional, and related occupations were held by women, although women's median earnings were still lower than men's, at $600 a week for women, or 81 percent of the men's median weekly earnings of $743.

More women have been rising to key marketing positions in U.S. companies. With extensive experience in brand management, Fiona Dias became vice president of marketing for the Frito-Lay Division of PepsiCo, Inc.; then chief marketing officer of Stick Networks, a new company producing Internet appliances; and eventually held the position of senior vice president of marketing for Circuit City Stores, Inc. Nina E. McLemore, founder of Liz Claiborne Accessories, proved to be a marketing genius and later became president of Regent Capital Management.

According to a growing body of management studies, women executives are rated higher by bosses, peers, and subordinates than their male counterparts in a variety of areas, including producing high-quality work, goal setting, and mentoring. However, one study showed that male CEOs and senior vice presidents received high ratings if they were forceful and assertive and lower ratings if they were cooperative and empathetic, while female CEOs received lower ratings for being assertive and higher ratings when they were cooperative. Perceptions change slowly at the top of the corporation.

It is particularly important for women to have mentors, not only because women are markedly underrepresented in top levels of management in larger companies, but also to receive knowledge only a member of the club can pass on. Women in management in large corporations often identify "a male-dominated corporate culture" as an obstacle to success. Some companies make a concerted effort to remove obstacles to women's advancement into corporate management through programs such as awareness training for men. Others set goals for promoting higher percentages of women.

Studies have been conducted to identify companies with woman-friendly corporate cultures. Factors considered included numbers of women in key executive positions and on the board of directors, specific efforts to help women advance, and sensitivity to the complexities of the work-family dilemma. Companies such as American Express, Avon, Baxter International, CBS, Corning, Dayton Hudson, Gannett, Honeywell, IBM, Johnson & Johnson, Kelly Services, Kemper, Merck, Monsanto, Pitney Bowes, Reader's Digest, Security Pacific Bank, Square D, and U.S. West, among others, have been acknowledged for their progressive practices in this area. These companies represent a wide variety of industries. Women have fared well in computer companies, entering in substantial numbers when their skills were much needed at the birth of the industry, but other companies in this group are from old, conservative industries such as banking and electrical manufacturing. These companies reversed some of their traditional practices to become more woman friendly.

Though women have had to work hard to prove themselves, every successful woman changes a few minds. Women's networks in companies often help other women learn the ropes. It is important for young women aspiring to management positions to be aware of how women are faring at the companies that are making them offers.

Questions to ask at interviews might include: What percentage of women hold top-management posts? What percentage hold middle-management posts? Do company benefits include extended leaves, flex-time, and day care assistance? The best offer for a new graduate may not come from a woman-friendly company but from a company offering excellent training and development opportunities. Trade-offs are always present in job offers. Both men and women should carefully consider and define their short- and long-range goals before entering the job market. This is not to say that goals should remain inflexible, but rather that a clear understanding of personal priorities is necessary.

CHIEF EXECUTIVE OFFICERS

The chief executive officers in large traditional U.S. companies have a number of attributes in common. Many come from wealthy families or ones in which the heads of the households were corporate managers, successful professionals, or graduates of top schools such as Yale, Princeton, and Harvard. The next-largest group attended Big Ten schools. Some attended military schools. Almost all hold bachelor's degrees, and many have one or more graduate degrees. Most CEOs are married with children. A large number enjoy sports, particularly golf and tennis.

CEOs have come up from a variety of functional areas, including finance/accounting, merchandising/marketing, engineering/technical, production/manufacturing, and the legal department. Most CEOs have worked for more than one company. Movement from one company to another occurs as boards recruit executives to lead companies through restructuring. In general, CEOs are multitalented, versatile people. There is precious little room at the top, and most new graduates hardly expect to become CEOs of large corporations. Still, the backgrounds of CEOs give some hints about the types of people who have scaled the heights in the past.

RESOURCES FOR MANAGERS

Three of the most useful resources for professional managers are company training and continuing education, professional organizations, and marketing periodicals and professional journals.

Management Training and Development

Management training and development is an indispensable ingredient in the success formula for marketing professionals. Without solid training and development opportunities, individuals can become stagnant early in their careers.

A job applicant should ask, "What kind of training and development will the company provide if I accept this position?" To meet training needs, some companies are allowing employees to select the pace of training that occurs both inside and outside the work environment. This partnership enables ambitious employees to have more control over training opportunities and to advance at their own rate. In addition to the traditional classroom lectures, company training programs employ technologies such as interactive video, computer-based training, and television courses. *The National Directory of Corporate Training Programs* (Elliott Bard Ray) provides information on such programs and the companies that offer them.

Formal training programs for managers and professionals are offered through business schools. Major restructuring in corporations has caused the emphasis of executive training to be placed on organizational transformation rather than personal development. Business schools are offering more custom programs designed for specific corporations. These programs, as well as in-house programs, are geared to meet specific goals or to transform corporate culture. General Electric, for example, sent managers to a program to learn how to develop markets in the fast-growing economies of Asia. Ford used management development to encourage closer cooperation across disciplines—that is, to create more product-oriented marketing people. Cigna Corporation used team-building activities to tackle real company problems, culminating in recommendations to senior management.

Going to work for a company that offers its employees training and development programs and support should be a central career objective. Along those lines, continuing education programs offered through colleges and universities enable individuals to increase their chances of promotion.

Many companies pay tuition costs for job-related courses, even entire M.B.A. programs. An M.B.A. is helpful, and often necessary, for advancing through management ranks. Regardless of the type of training and continuing education that an employer provides, professionals are responsible for making the most of their own training and career development opportunities.

Training opportunities are also available through memberships in professional organizations. By joining as a student, one can take advantage of some early training opportunities and gain a competitive edge.

Professional Management Organizations

Participation in local, national, and international professional organizations is beneficial both to marketing professionals and to students. The organizations provide the opportunity for communication among members at meetings and conferences. In addition, much current information is disseminated through advanced training and seminars sponsored by the organizations. Many offer placement services for members and for new college graduates. The price of membership for students is greatly reduced in most cases.

A good source for names and addresses of professional organizations is the *Encyclopedia of Associations*, which is published annually and can be found in the reference section of the library. Information includes names, addresses, and phone numbers of professional associations; the date they were founded; the number of current members; a description of the membership; and publications, if any.

In addition to the organizations related to specific areas of marketing, as listed in other chapters of this book, many marketing managers hold memberships in the following associations:

American Management Association
1601 Broadway
New York, NY 10019
amanet.org

American Marketing Association
311 S. Wacker Dr., Ste. 5800
Chicago, IL 60606
marketingpower.com

Asia Pacific Management Association
Starhub Centre, Kaplan City Campus
51 Cuppage Rd.
Singapore 229469
apmi.edu.sg

Sales and Marketing Executives International
PO Box 1390
Sumas, WA 98295
smei.org

Management Newsletters and Journals

Many professional associations publish newsletters and journals. Marketing periodicals are ideal sources of general information. An impressive list can be obtained from *Ulrich's International Periodicals Directory*, held in the reference section of the library. It is published annually by R. R. Bowker Company, New York and London. A good many marketing periodicals can be tracked down in public and university libraries. Most marketing professionals subscribe to several periodicals to keep current and gain professional insights. Also included in many newsletters and journals are classified ads posting job openings. Of course, endless resources for managers are online.

OPPORTUNITIES FOR MANAGERS

Demand for new managers will vary considerably from industry to industry in the next ten years. Primarily owing to the uncertain economy both nationally and internationally, many industries are applying more stringent controls to their budgets. Business and information services are expected to experience strong growth, along with advertising, sales promotion, and public relations agencies. Much of this growth in service agencies is due to outsourcing, a trend among companies toward contracting work to outside agencies, many of which are in other countries, and it is likely to continue. This growth will create many new opportunities for marketing managers, both in the United States and abroad.

Executive search firms report record amounts of billings for senior managers and the most active CEO market they have ever seen. The most pronounced rise in demand is for marketing executives, frequently considered to be the only true generalists in the company, because of their overall industry perspective. Consequently, they are in demand even in technology-oriented companies and particularly in the telecommunications and software industries.

As a group, advertising, marketing, promotions, public relations, and sales managers positions are expected to rise 12 percent over the decade from 2006 through 2016, according to the *National Employment Matrix*, published by the U.S. Bureau of Labor Statistics.

MANAGEMENT COMPENSATION

Because of negative publicity about extremely high salaries for top executives and also the need to cut back expenses, executive compensation is undergoing some changes. Many boards of directors are hiring pay consultants to help determine what their people are worth. A trend to link CEOs' paychecks to corporate performance has taken hold in some areas.

Median annual earnings for advertising and promotion managers in May 2006 were $73,060; for marketing managers, $98,720; for sales managers, $91,560; and for public relations managers, $97,540, according to the Bureau of Labor Statistics.

Salary is not always the most significant part of the compensation package. Stock holdings in the company can amount to millions, sometimes billions.

Management compensation varies widely depending on the industry, level of management, size of budget, scope of responsibility, and the individual's expertise and reputation. CEOs of nonprofit organizations may earn lower pay. Though women executives in sales and management earn less than men, there is indication that the base salary for women executives is increasing at a faster rate than that of men. Benefits such as stock options and long-term compensation vary greatly as well. Each management position and its compensation package must be evaluated individually.

CHAPTER 9

CAREERS IN GLOBAL MARKETING

By 2008, the global marketplace was a spaghetti bowl of intersections and interactions: international trade agreements, international banks and other financial organizations, multinational corporations, intergovernmental projects, and a fresh batch of new and largely independent commercial exchanges are crisscrossing the globe twenty-four hours a day, every day.

From a business standpoint, the world is dynamically connected through increasingly advanced communications technology and the now fundamental platform of the Internet. More opportunities for marketing products globally exist now than we ever could have imagined. It seems as though everyone in Canada and the United States knows someone who is going to study Arabic, Chinese, Hindu, Russian, or Urdu.

One approach that companies are using today in new-product development is assembling geographically dispersed global teams whose members differ by culture and language. Technologies such as videoconferencing, audio conferencing, and e-mail enable team members to communicate with each other around the world.

The new millennium has witnessed the emergence of China as a global trading partner with preferred trading status. Direct foreign investment is on the rise, with U.S. companies investing in other countries, and other countries investing in the United States. Argentina, Malaysia, Mexico, and Singapore are major beneficiaries of an influx of foreign capital.

Global marketing is a complicated field requiring in-depth cultural and demographic knowledge of potential markets. Global marketing—also called international marketing, multinational marketing, and transnational marketing—comprises the activities of organizations that engage in exchanges across national borders. Both business and nonbusiness organizations such as charities, religious organizations, and universities engage in global marketing. Whether selling products, soliciting donations, or recruiting students, these organizations operate in a global environment that has its own rules and requirements. Business organizations, whether U.S. based or headquartered abroad, are attempting to tap into the unprecedented growth in global marketing.

THE IMPACT OF FOREIGN COMPETITION ON U.S. CORPORATIONS

Competition from European and Asian markets has forced U.S. companies to think globally and become importers instead of exporters. Since the 1992 economic integration of the European Community, many trade barriers have been removed between countries. Many U.S. companies in Europe have taken advantage of this opportunity, including Coca-Cola Company, Ford Motor Company, Hewlett-Packard Company, IBM, and Merck & Company, all of which have had successful operations in Europe for years. In Japan, Amway, Disney Company, DuPont Company, and McDonald's Corporation have prospered. Toys "R" Us has stores in Canada, Europe, Hong Kong, Japan, and Singapore. To be successful, retailers must have the kind of format, supplier relationships, and expertise to operate with success globally.

As foreign economies mature, they create enormous markets for construction equipment, telecommunications products, and a host of other goods and services. Many U.S. corporations have built or bought factories in Eastern Europe. The attraction of Eastern Europe includes its large consumer market and educated labor force. In the Western Hemisphere, the passage of the North American Free Trade Agreement wiped out some protective tariffs and moved to create a unified North American economy. Free trade has both positive and negative economic aspects for the countries involved, and these agreements affect the nature of the global marketplace and create new and different kinds of opportunities.

CONSUMER DEMAND AND ITS IMPACT ON GLOBAL MARKETING

The developed countries of the world offer markets for U.S. products, but these markets are not yet growing as significantly as many entrepreneurs and others have hoped. It is true, however, that 77 percent of our global population lives in developing countries. Hundreds of millions of consumers in Asia will enter or approach the ranks of the middle class within the next decades and will provide a growing market for consumer goods. Eastern Europe contains millions of consumers needing clothes, appliances, and many other basic items. In Latin America, an awareness of international brands exists, so the demand is there, and beginning the marketing processes for many products may be somewhat easier. Cultural barriers may, however, affect the introduction of certain products. People interested in careers in global marketing should broaden their perspective to include preparation to enter these diverse and growing markets.

Creating brands is as important worldwide as it is in the United States. Barclays Global Investors, one of the world's largest money managers, hired as head of its global marketing a Canadian, Kathy Taylor, who was committed to using worldwide media to establish Barclays as a brand with all the loyalty and name recognition of the most familiar and popular of U.S. and Canadian consumer products.

HOW COMPANIES ARE INVOLVED IN FOREIGN MARKETS

Companies have four primary options for entering foreign markets:

Foreign Operations
Joint Ventures
Exporting
Licensing

These options differ in many complex ways, but especially in the levels of financial commitment and risk involved.

Foreign Operations and Joint Ventures. Multinational companies commit a great deal of resources to establishing operations in foreign countries, and they often take on a lot of risk. While they run the risk of consumers' rejecting their products, they also face political risks, including confiscation of their property by the government of the host country. To counter this risk, some companies enter into joint ventures as a way of tapping into foreign markets. The government of the host country or a locally owned firm may go into partnership with a foreign company interested in entering the local market. More countries are requiring this type of joint venture as a condition for entering their markets.

Exporting. An alternative to foreign-based operations is exporting. Exporting accomplishes the objective of selling in foreign markets without the large risk inherent in on-site operations. The opening of markets in Eastern countries, along with the increasing demand for U.S. consumer products worldwide, has made exporting even more enticing. Many companies establish export departments and sell directly to foreign firms. These departments contact foreign buyers, conduct marketing research, and arrange distribution and export documentation.

Foreign distribution may be through manufacturers' representatives, import jobbers, dealers, wholesalers, or retailers who function overseas in the same way as their counterparts in the United States. As companies become more proficient at exporting, they may begin to explore possibilities for foreign operations.

Rather than directly exporting, companies may work through intermediaries. Trading companies are private or government-owned organizations that buy and sell products in much the same way as merchant wholesalers and wholesale dealers and merchandise brokers. These companies may place orders with exporters for their own accounts or for a client. Some of these companies offer a complete range of services to their clients, encompassing importing, exporting, storing, transporting, and distribution through intermediaries.

An ongoing headache for small and midsize exporters has been financing. Many banks do not cater to the complexities of operating in foreign markets, and some are unwilling to spend the hours it takes to set up letters of credit. Traditionally, regional and foreign-based banks have handled export financing. Export trading companies take title to exports and complete transactions for their clients by shipping the goods and collecting payment. Various financial services companies help to facilitate more export trade and, at the same time, provide many job opportunities.

Foreign Licensing. Still another option, particularly attractive to small companies that cannot afford to invest capital in foreign operations, is foreign licensing. A company will license its concept, which can be a product or a process, to a foreign entity that already has local facilities and understands the market. In return, the business receives royalties that can range from an eighth of a percent to 15 percent or more of sales, but every contract varies in many different details. In addition to royalties, the company may get valuable feedback regarding R&D and marketing from the foreign licensee.

MORE ABOUT CAREERS IN GLOBAL MARKETING

Careers in global marketing do not necessarily mean extensive travel. Most multinational companies prefer to fill positions in foreign countries with citizens of that country and may even be required to do so. The practicality is obvious. Natives speak the language, understand the customs, are paid on a local scale, and do a better job of representing the company than would foreigners.

More than likely, recent graduates in international business, especially at entry-level positions, will be based in the United States while dealing with companies abroad. Though lacking in the glamour desired by many young single people, positions in the United States do not present such complications as chronic homesickness or the need to find English-language education for school-age children. There are many reasons to enter the field of global marketing, including challenges and growing opportunities. However, it is important to understand that although upper-level managers may be posted abroad or travel abroad frequently, entry- and lower-level personnel will probably be based stateside.

Companies headquartered in one country become multinational when they begin to produce and sell goods in other countries. When their operations extend around the world, they are referred to as global enterprises. Much groundwork must be done to select and enter foreign markets successfully. The economic, technological, sociocultural, and political environments in which the business must operate differ widely from country to country, making the activities of global marketing, as detailed in the following sections, considerably more complex.

Global Marketing Research. Although global marketing research professionals perform roughly the same duties as those described in Chapter 2, their work is appreciably more complicated. They must first obtain information from secondary sources. Useful data may be gathered from such organizations as the Organization for Economic Cooperation and Development, the United Nations, the U.N. Food and Agriculture Organization, the U.N. World Health Organization, and regional trading blocs, such as the Andean Common Market, the Association of Southeast Asian Nations, and the European Community.

In addition, governments in foreign countries and U.S. embassies can provide useful information. Researchers can also consult nongovernment sources such as banks, international trade clubs, and executives of companies doing business in the country. However, much of this information may have been estimated or crudely compiled and must be carefully analyzed to determine whether primary data should be collected.

Collecting primary data is even trickier than analyzing the secondary data. While many marketing research techniques may be adapted for use in developed countries, they may be totally unsuitable for use in developing countries with high illiteracy rates, unreliable postal and telephone service, language barriers, and a general suspicion of people asking a battery of questions. To determine which techniques would be appropriate for use in a particular country, marketing researchers must be familiar with the economic, technological, sociocultural, and political factors within that country. Language skills are invaluable, since many pertinent sources of information will be in the home language(s) of that particular country.

Global Product Management. The decisions that must be made regarding products to be marketed abroad are complex. Members of the project management team have three alternatives for product development. Short descriptions of each follow:

• **Product Standardization.** The identical product is sold both at home and abroad. This is workable only if the product is suitable for foreign markets. It is the least costly of the three alternatives.

• **Product Adaptation.** A product is modified or adapted to suit local tastes and uses.

• **Product Innovation.** A product is especially designed for each foreign market.

The team must also grapple with name, distribution, packaging, pricing, and promotion decisions.

Global Promotion. Advertising, sales promotion, publicity, and personal selling must take into account attitudes of consumers, competitors, intermediaries, and governments. Clearly, whether an approach will be effective, or even allowed, depends on an accurate assessment of these attitudes. Global companies can use ad agencies in their home country, local agencies, or a global advertising agency with branches in numerous countries. United States–based ad agencies have been opening branches in foreign countries for many years. The employees in these branches are often hired from the local population. Personal selling is even more culture-bound than advertising. Therefore, sales of consumer products are conducted by local nationals who understand cultural preferences and etiquette in their country. Many manufacturers of expensive industrial products and pharmaceuticals employ U.S. sales representatives who work abroad, but they must study the habits and behaviors of their customers in order to perform at the desired level.

GLOBAL E-COMMERCE AND TELESERVICES

Opportunities created by advanced communications and Internet technology are global, but United States–based marketers are only beginning to capitalize on them. Part of the reason for the delay is that the majority of the market is in the United States, where there are more Internet users than in the rest of the world combined. Other factors include prohibitive government regulations and tariffs, poor infrastructure, high phone rates, and language differences.

Internet usage around the world is increasing rapidly. Strong consumer interest is being noted in China and Latin America, among other regions. Companies such as FedEx, Gateway, and Ford have led the way in global e-commerce, and thousands of others have followed. Websites and other corporate communications are routinely prepared with local language and cultural considerations.

Teleservices also provide opportunity for expansion into Europe and Asia, where steady growth in call centers is occurring. As is the case with other countries' call centers, United States–based call centers have had to address the wide range of cultures, languages, and currencies in Latin and South America, Europe, Asia, and other areas, as well as the varying public telecommunications infrastructures and Internet usage. Companies may begin by partnering with local consortia, external service providers, systems integrators, or consultancies to identify opportunities and the best ways to interface with customers. Websites can be used as a tool to support call center sales.

OPPORTUNITIES IN GLOBAL MARKETING

Demand in multinational companies is increasing for M.B.A.s and consultants with expertise in company restructuring and marketing strategy. Positions abroad are offered to those who have mastered their firm's domestic marketing operations and can speak the language and understand the customs of the country in which they will be based. Travel abroad is usually associated with high-level managers, managers or owners of advertising agencies with operations abroad, owners of export-import businesses, sales representatives of industrial and pharmaceutical products, and fashion coordinators and buyers for stores featuring foreign fashion lines. Foreign-based career opportunities are increasing as more corporations create and expand global operations.

Many U.S. and Canadian colleges and universities have developed programs of courses geared toward global marketing and are sponsoring more study abroad. Today, leading business schools are sending students overseas in their executive M.B.A. programs. Most programs abroad are conducted in partnership with local schools. The University of Chicago and Stanford's Thunderbird School of Management were some of the first business schools to prepare executive M.B.A. programs for international management. The University of Chicago pioneered by basing its entire program abroad. The program was designed to attract managers from other countries as well as those from the United States.

In the past, many M.B.A. students were sponsored by corporations, which helped pay tuition and allowed time off from work to attend classes. In spite of tighter training budgets, some of these programs prevail. Job applicants interested in positions abroad should inquire about such programs during the initial interviews. Further, many American employees abroad work for small firms, so opportunities with small companies should not be overlooked.

Foreign internships are available for American students wanting international experience. Students live and work in a foreign country as part of exchange programs that may last from six weeks to eighteen months. Students attracted to global marketing should become proficient in at least one other language and should systematically research and gather information on countries and industries of interest. The annual *Directory of Overseas Summer Jobs*, published by Peterson's Guides, Inc., is a useful resource held by most university libraries and career centers.

The demand for Americans to work in Asia has spiked, and opportunities exist in China, Japan, Malaysia, South Korea, and Taiwan. Additional information about these openings can be obtained from the individual consulates in major U.S. cities, as well as from their websites.

ADDITIONAL SOURCES OF INFORMATION

Anyone interested in international marketing can gain more information about the field from international marketing and trade associations such as the following:

American Association of Exporters and Importers
1050 Seventeenth St. NW
Washington, DC 20036
aaei.org

Mobile Marketing Association (Global)
1670 Broadway, Ste. 850
Denver, CO 80202
mmaglobal.com

United Nations International Trade Center (ITC)
United Nations Conference on Trade and Development (UNCTAD)
World Trade Organization (WTO)
Palais des Nations, 1211
Geneva 10
Switzerland

World Trade Centers Association
420 Lexington Ave., Ste. 518
New York, NY 10170
wtca.org

Several directories offer information on companies doing business abroad, including *Directory of American Firms Operating in Foreign Countries*, *Directory of European Retailers*, *Directory of Foreign Firms Operating in the U.S.*, *Principal International Businesses*, and *World Marketing Directory*. In addition, Surrey Books, Inc., has published *How to Get a Job in Europe*, by Robert Sanborn. This title is part of a series that also offers information on jobs in the Pacific Rim and in various cities around the United States. Another publication, *Almanac of International Jobs and Careers*, by Ronald L. Krannick and Caryl Rae Krannick, provides information on organizations abroad that hire U.S. citizens.

CHAPTER 10

CAREERS IN EDUCATION, CONSULTING, ENTREPRENEURSHIP, AND FRANCHISING

A marketing background often leads individuals to pursue careers in higher education, consulting, or entrepreneurship. Working in a corporate environment is not for everyone. Some people are mavericks who require greater autonomy in a work atmosphere. Many business students feel that operating their own businesses may be the best way to attain their goals but aren't certain that they can actually end up doing it.

A career is often an amalgam of work experience gleaned from varied positions and in many areas. An illustration is the career of Elliot S. Schreiber, president and CEO of the Alliance for Converging Technologies, a research and consulting firm focusing on strategies in a digital economy. Along with stints in university teaching and international consulting, he held executive positions in three industries over a twenty-year period in sales, advertising, marketing strategy, brand management, and corporate communications. With that varied and successful background, Schreiber became a valuable asset to a research and consulting firm.

The careers described in this chapter are not for beginners but can be viable goals with the proper education and experience. Most successful entrepreneurs have worked for others and gained needed knowledge and skills before striking out on their own. This chapter mines some interesting career alternatives.

MARKETING EDUCATION

Marketing educators teach in many types of educational settings, with varying requirements attached to each. The most common settings are colleges and universities. Training and education is also a part of most marketing managerial positions.

Graduate Degree Requirements

Professional educators in the field of marketing attain positions in two- and four-year colleges that have marketing courses or marketing programs of study. A master's degree in marketing is usually sufficient to qualify for a teaching position in a community college. Depending on supply and demand, a doctorate may be required and is always preferred.

A doctorate in marketing is always a prerequisite for tenure-track positions in four-year colleges and universities. Earning one's doctorate demands a serious commitment of both time and money. After a four-year bachelor's program, a master's program, usually requiring approximately two years of full-time study, must be undertaken. Completion of a master's-level program, however, does not always guarantee admission to a doctoral program.

To be accepted, applicants for doctoral programs must have the ability to successfully complete graduate courses in marketing, and they must also achieve a high enough score on the Graduate Management Admissions Test (GMAT) and demonstrate the potential for conducting original research. Doctoral programs require at least two years of full-time course work and seminars, along with the design and completion of a doctoral dissertation. This can be a lengthy process, and a committee must approve each stage before the candidate may go on. A review of the literature, design of the project, data gathering or laboratory experimentation, and an analysis of results can take well over a year to complete.

When recent Ph.D. recipients apply for positions with prestigious and well-known universities, they will find that the reputation of their alma mater, its doctoral program, and its professors will have an influence on whether or not they are accepted. Students seeking doctorates should carefully evaluate a school and its program before entering. Finding a major professor who shares the student's research interests and who is well known in the field can make doctoral study easier and more valuable. It can also make the student more marketable when entering the job market.

Some universities are famous in their fields, and marketing departments in some universities are well known both for the erudition and leadership of their senior faculty and for famous alumni who have gone on to make names for themselves in the industry. Usually the leading academic and commercial gurus of the industry are well represented among the keynote speakers of the major conventions each year. These men and women have an enormous effect on the culture of America, in both measurable and immeasurable ways. Their students are often disciples to their philosophies and methodologies, and they may influence thousands of graduates during a lifetime career.

As the demand for marketing professionals increases, the demand for marketing educators increases along with it. Demand may vary by area of specialization. Doctoral candidates may concentrate in marketing research, marketing management, advertising and promotion, public relations, international marketing, interactive Internet marketing, international purchasing and production, and so forth.

Selection criteria may include the applicant's master's thesis, choice of dissertation topic, and other earlier research, publications, evaluations by professors, and experience outside the doctoral program, such as previous employment in commercial marketing areas. Evaluations of the applicant's teaching experience, if any, may also be considered, since many doctoral students will teach undergraduate marketing classes as part of their graduate assistantships.

In addition, recent Ph.D. graduates are often invited to stay on as instructors or assistant professors in the same school where they have just completed their Ph.D. work.

Responsibilities and Advancement

In two-year schools, instructors primarily teach, but they also may be expected to publish articles in their fields. University professors normally have lighter teaching loads but are expected to publish articles and books in their fields in order to be eligible for promotion and tenure. In addition, both instructors and professors are evaluated on their related service to their schools, which usually includes serving on various committees and can involve fund-raising and other duties as well.

Assistant professors are promoted to associate professor and then full professor. Leading college professors often enter administrative positions such as marketing department chair or dean. Dean of undergraduate or graduate business studies, or dean of the college of business administration, as well as other deanships on a college campus, are sometimes filled by former marketing professors.

It is not unusual for professors to earn additional income outside the university as authors, speakers, consultants, and sometimes entrepreneurs. For example, Super Lube, a large quick-oil-change franchise, was started by two Florida State University professors—one in marketing and the other in real estate.

MARKETING CONSULTING

Marketing consultants are problem solvers with extensive experience in both marketing and an area of expertise, such as marketing strategy, marketing research, advertising, sales, or merchandising. Large companies spend millions on consulting and research services. Consulting firms such as Arthur Andersen provide these services.

As companies grow, shrink, restructure, and expand into national, international, and global operations, they employ consultants to help with these transitions. Businesses and industries hire consultants to help plan marketing strategies and solve problems when strategies go awry. Consulting firms and independent consultants in the United States and Canada are listed in the *Consultants and Consulting Organizations Directory*, found in the reference section of most large libraries. Companies hire marketing consultants mostly in the areas of marketing strategy, market and product research, and feasibility studies.

What Consultants Do

Since consultants work for many clients, they are exposed to different methods of solving problems and to a variety of valuable sources of information. Consultants use their diverse experience to analyze and solve problems for clients. Armed with knowledge of what works and what doesn't in a variety of situations, the consultant can make recommendations that save time and money. Most consultants have broad freedom over their time and resources. Whether they freelance, ply their trade in small companies, or are members of large consulting firms, they generally work independently with individual clients.

In order to be rehired by a client, a consultant must demonstrate the ability to help solve the client's problems in both creative and cost-effective ways. Consulting is not the job for someone who wants to work less and avoid the nine-to-five routine. Longer, though less routine hours are required for successful consulting. Client companies often impose hard-to-meet deadlines and expect unrealistic results.

Trends in Consulting

Corporate downsizing and growth in the Internet economy has created considerable demand for outside consulting work. Consultants with technological skills in Web-enabled customer relationship management, supply-chain management, and wireless technology systems are in demand.

Change management and corporate reengineering are particular areas of demand in the consulting business. Because of reengineering in Europe and in developing economies around the world, there are many opportunities for consultants who want to work abroad.

At one time, consulting was narrow in scope, and most consultants worked alone. Today, consultants also team up with managers and work together as a unit to analyze and solve problems.

Companies that have downsized their management positions use consultants to complete projects that would have been done in-house. Assignments may be short term or may last years and involve crucial extended strategy, operations, organization, and technology management. Consultants working on longer projects can often be paid high fees, but organizational executives are also expecting more for their money in terms of positive results, especially in tight financial periods.

Finding Clients

A consultant competes with other consultants for jobs. Though the use of consultants may significantly benefit a company, it is not required for doing business and is one of the first budget items to be crossed out in hard times. Therefore, consultants must sell their services aggressively. They use a variety of promotional avenues to obtain clients: personal relationships and networking, participation in seminars, mailing and phoning, door-to-door selling, advertising, marketing agents, and public relations companies.

Unless a company is rehiring a consultant who has worked for it previously, it will usually screen and interview several consultants. For large contracts, company representatives will visit recent client sites and ask for evidence that the consultant produced results. Who is hired depends on a range of factors including the following:

- **Compatibility.** The company managers and consultants must get along personally, since they will usually be working together as a team.
- **Reputation.** The quality of the consultant's references, including other companies for whom the consultant has completed a similar assignment, is another primary consideration. Successful work, ethical behavior, and professional integrity are all relevant. Although consultants may work for competing companies, consulting contracts often stipulate that they may not disclose privileged company information or work for a directly competing firm for a certain period after the project is completed.
- **Experience.** Not only the number of years of experience but also the quality of that experience are considered.
- **Proven Results.** Achieving a history of accomplishments that can be quantified and verified is essential to building a consulting business.

Sometimes consultants hire consulting broker firms to obtain clients. Brokers normally earn 25 to 40 percent of what the consultant earns on the initial contact with the hiring company and less on subsequent contacts. Consulting fees vary widely, depending on the scope and complexity of the project and the reputation of the consultant. Well-established, successful consultants rarely go without employment, but building a solid reputation and clientele requires diligence over a span of years.

Working for a Consulting Firm

Because people are the primary resource in consulting companies, everyone in large consulting companies gets involved in recruiting new employees. In general, professionals who become consultants have at least two to four years of experience in the field, a college degree, and often an M.B.A. or doctorate. For example, an M.B.A. with a degree in international marketing from Thunderbird, or another graduate business school that emphasizes international trade, may work two to four years in the field and then apply to a marketing management consulting firm, or become an independent consultant.

Top consulting firms tend to hire graduates from the best business schools and then train them. These firms typically also offer summer internships to promising candidates and evaluate these recruits before offering them permanent employment.

Work in large consulting firms is characterized by pressure, long hours, travel, and high turnover. Many of these firms are partnerships that follow an up-or-out policy; that is, consultants have from five to seven years to make partner. If they fail, they are out. Only one in five who begin work with a large company is expected to make partner. Many people opt for consulting with large firms for the training and experience first and then go out on their own by choice. Many consulting firms are based in the Northeast and in California. Large U.S. firms have branches throughout the United States and Canada, and possibly in Europe, Asia, Africa, Latin and South America, and Australia. Marketing consulting firms headquartered in other countries, most recently notably in Asian countries, have established branches in the United States and Canada as well.

Companies often retain consultants on a continuing basis, so consulting work can be long term. Entry-level consulting work in large companies is often geared to market research. As junior consultants or associates demonstrate the analytic, interpersonal, and motivational skills required for success in the job, they are promoted to the position of case team leader or senior consultant. In this capacity, a consultant supervises a small team, normally working on one or two cases at a time. Two or three years later, a senior consultant who is performing well may be promoted to consulting manager. As manager, a consultant leads a consulting team on high-priority client projects. Once promoted to junior partner, and finally senior partner or director, the consultant will be dedicated primarily to marketing the firm and its services.

Earnings vary widely for independent consultants, but the U.S. Department of Labor reports that self-employed management consultants earned a median income of $76,600 annually as of May 2006. Employed consultants, working for consulting firms, earned a median income of $58.97 per hour, and analyst consultants working for consulting firms earned a median of $36.83 hourly. Customer service representative consultants working for consulting firms received a median income of $14.91 per hour.

Independent Consulting

The number of small consulting operations with no more than three people has increased over the years as more retirees open part-time or full-time businesses and as laid-off workers decide to go into business for themselves. Estimates are that only one in five is able to succeed for the long run. Success will depend in part on how well consultants can use information technology, especially electronic networks, to gain up-to-the-minute data.

Independent consulting can be done on a full-time or part-time basis. Many university professors do consulting to supplement their salaries. Retired executives or executives between jobs are in demand as consultants. A marketing-strategy consultant should book solid experience as a successful marketing manager in a position fairly high up in an organization before seeking independent status.

Consultants are usually well paid when they have work, but continually maintaining a reliable cash flow and paying the bills requires steady work. A rule of thumb is that self-employed consultants must earn approximately 50 percent more than their large-firm counterparts to cover the costs of doing business and the benefits usually provided by an employer, such as health insurance, paid holidays and vacations, travel expenses, office space, supplies and equipment, clerical help, and telephone expenses.

ADDITIONAL SOURCES OF INFORMATION FOR CONSULTANTS

Numerous publications are available to people interested in consulting as a profession. Consultants are listed in a number of directories, including *Consultants and Consulting Organizations Directory* and *Dun's Consultants Directory*, housed in the reference section of most university and large city libraries. *Consultants News* and *Journal of Management Consulting* are periodicals covering up-to-date information in the field. A selection of associations for consultants follows:

Association of Management Consulting Firms
380 Lexington Ave., Ste. 1700
New York, NY 10168
amcf.org

Institute of Management Consultants
2025 M St., Ste. 800
Washington, DC 20036
imcusa.org

Professional and Technical Consultants Association
PO Box 2261
Santa Clara, CA 95055
patca.org

ONLINE JOB SERVICES FOR INDEPENDENT CONTRACTORS

According to the Economic Policy Institute, more than a third of the U.S. workforce is made up of nonstandard workers, which include temporary workers, on-call workers, day laborers, leased workers, self-employed people, and independent contractors. To tap into this reservoir of talent, the Internet offers skills auctions, job sites, resume sites, and recruiters. The auctions offer independent contractors bids for their services, though not always at the pay rates they would like. Internet companies such as Monster.com, and Marketingjobs.com provide job descriptions and ads, placement tips, and other useful information.

ENTREPRENEURSHIP

Confidence in themselves and their ideas is what propels entrepreneurs into business against all odds. Kate Spade and her husband, Andy, used his $35,000 in savings to produce the high-fashion handbags that women purchase for hundreds of dollars in upscale department stores. Kate Spade Inc. today operates its own retail stores, and Kate Spade bags are carried by some of the most prestigious specialty shops in the world.

Many people start new businesses every year. Some are those who lost their jobs as a result of downsizing, but most are individuals seeking a better quality of life than they are able to attain working for someone else. Current-day entrepreneurs are characterized by being better educated and having more sophisticated businesses than in previous years.

New start-ups in e-commerce—the so-called dot-coms—were plentiful in the late 1990s, but many failed with the downward correction of the economy. The perception that building an Internet business is easy and cheap is false. In today's economy, capital isn't as readily obtained, technology is complicated, and skilled employees are scarce, but a steady stream of successful e-businesses rolls on.

An early success was digIT Interactive Inc., which became one of Canada's top fifty Web-services companies before selling to Nurun, Canada's largest Web-services company and a global player. Correctly anticipating the problems that small Web-services companies would face in an uncertain economic future with competition becoming stiffer and more global, digIT's four major shareholders made a smart decision by selling.

Many successful online companies provide consulting or business services to other businesses. Less expensive computer and telecommunications equipment has been a contributing factor here.

Small businesses help to sustain the U.S. economy. According to the Bureau of Labor Statistics, small businesses account for about half of nonfarm, nongovernmental employment and about half of the private-sector output in the United States. During the 1990s, small businesses generated three-quarters of the growth in jobs. High-tech and Internet-related start-ups are on the rise and are creating enough new jobs to keep employment within start-ups rising. An explanation for this record is that many high-tech start-ups grow more rapidly, having access to broader customer markets, and many are employing one hundred people within the first year or so.

About 5 percent of the small businesses create most of the jobs. However, apart from job creation, entrepreneurial companies spur large companies to make innovations in products and to create new markets. The impact on technology made by Bill Gates and the impact on retailing made by the late Sam Walton, founder of Wal-Mart, are outstanding examples. Realistically, most of today's small businesses provide only a modest living for their owners, and the majority of new, small business start-ups will go out of business within the first three years.

Entrepreneurs are those individuals who are willing to assume the risks of starting their own businesses. Given these risks, which are formidable, why do they do it? Some reasons frequently given are to use skills or ability, to gain control over one's life, to build for the family, for the challenge, to live in a particular location, to gain respect or recognition, to earn lots of money, and to fulfill others' expectations. In the United States, and in many countries abroad, women have been starting businesses at twice the rate of men. More and more African-Americans likewise are launching their own companies. A black business network of powerful contacts is catalyzing economic growth in such areas as communications, entertainment, and consumer goods.

Entrepreneurs Start with a Good Idea

The demand for a product or service creates an opportunity for prospective entrepreneurs. Understanding that consumers in the twenty-first century want to be educated, be entertained, preserve the environment, be good parents, stay healthy, and feel rich, clever entrepreneurs have designed products to meet these needs.

Big business leaves many needs unmet and market niches untapped. Entrepreneurs go against the odds every time they start a new business, but that doesn't stop many from succeeding. Independent entrepreneurs find a market niche, develop a product, and market it as do large companies. A copious amount of knowledge and tireless effort are required to develop a successful small business.

Succeeding as an Entrepreneur

Owning a start-up business is an all-consuming job. Because of the substantial investment of time and money and the high risk of failure, an entrepreneur must have a total commitment to the business, a tolerance for hard work, good health, and financial backing.

The prospective entrepreneur usually seeks financial backing from relatives, friends, and lending institutions. Entrepreneurs also usually put a good bit of their own money into their businesses. If they have developed an impressive business plan, with a sound and realistic potential of making a considerable profit, they may be successful in getting financial backing from outside sources such as banks or venture capitalists.

Venture capital firms are usually groups of investors who extend financial backing to start-up companies in exchange for part ownership of the company, depending on the terms of each arrangement. Usually the venture capital firm wants to protect its investment by having considerable say in how the company is run. Meanwhile, many entrepreneurs have taken on the risk of starting their own businesses in order to have total freedom to run them as they see fit, and when this is the case, the entrepreneur attempts to go it alone, avoiding capital with strings attached.

While securing financial backing is often a formidable stumbling block for entrepreneurs, more than money is required to make a business thrive. Once finances are arranged, an entrepreneur begins to implement the business plan. In most small businesses, the owner is responsible for planning, accounting, purchasing, producing, marketing, staffing, and overall management, so a general knowledge of all the activities of business is necessary. Above all else, an entrepreneur must be a salesperson extraordinaire—first selling the idea to raise capital to start the company, and then selling the company and its future to prospective employees, and finally selling the product to consumers who are constantly bombarded with ideas for new and better products. Entrepreneurs should be thoroughly aware of market and economic conditions if they hope to succeed, and these conditions are in constant flux.

Preparing for Entrepreneurship

Can a person be taught to be an entrepreneur? Probably not, but what can be taught are the skills needed for an entrepreneur to be successful. In response to demand, business schools are adding more courses and encouraging more student participation in entrepreneurial competitions. Some schools offer comprehensive entrepreneurship programs, usually in the form of a concentration of electives. Course work focuses on the financing of a new business and the commercialization of new products. The best preparation, however, is outside the classroom, working for a company in the same industry that the prospective entrepreneur is planning eventually to enter.

ADDITIONAL SOURCES OF INFORMATION FOR SMALL BUSINESSES

Usually small family businesses employ family members in key positions, and if the business has a board of directors, they too are often family members. In such a situation, the question of where to get objective advice on business matters arises. The Small Business Administration (SBA), with offices in all major cities, is a highly recommended source of information for people who want to start their own businesses or need help once they have set up shop. Numerous brochures published by the SBA are available in SBA offices and can also be requested by mail. These brochures explain how to develop a business plan, acquire financing, market products, and much more. In addition, many helpful books have been written on managing small businesses, and some consultants specialize in offering services to small business owners who can afford them.

Information and assistance for small business owners can be obtained by contacting the following organizations:

Chamber of Commerce of the United States
1615 H St. NW
Washington, DC 20062
uschamber.com

National Association of Small Business Investment Companies
666 11th St. NW, Ste.750
Washington, DC 20001
nasbic.org

National Association of Women Business Owners
8405 Greensboro Dr., Ste. 800
McLean, VA 22102
nawbo.org

National Business Association
5151 Beltline Rd., Ste. 1150
Dallas, TX 75254
nationalbusiness.com

FRANCHISING

Many people want to own a small business but have neither an original idea nor the business acumen to start a business from scratch, so they buy a franchise. A franchise is an agreement between a small business owner and a parent company that gives the owner the right to sell the company's product (goods or services) under conditions agreed on by both. The store itself is also called a franchise. Many small retail stores are franchises, including fast-food stores, gas stations, and print shops. Statistics show that the proportionate number of failures among franchises is significantly less than small business failures in general. The reason for this difference is that franchises enjoy special advantages over other small business operations.

Franchising is big business in the United States, with more than 767,000 franchises reported by the U.S. government in 2006 and an estimate of more than eighteen million jobs generated by these stores. All types of people opt for franchise ownership and for all types of reasons.

- Bill Anderson was on the road almost three hundred days a year and used Mail Boxes Etc. for shipping during off-hours. He was so impressed with the service that he opened his own, and then another.
- When Anthony Cracolici was terminated from a job he'd held for twenty years, he and his wife attended a small business expo where they discovered Happy & Healthy Products, Inc., a company that sells all-natural frozen dessert bars. They bought a franchise and became master distributors, the highest level of franchise ownership for the company.
- Tammy Cassman worked for years in retail sales before opening a Fastframe picture-framing franchise, with corporate headquarters offering her training and even helping her clean and organize her store.
- Ron McBride used his experience in tax law at the Internal Revenue Service to help him succeed with his Triple Check Income Tax Service franchise, to which he added a Triple Check Financial Services franchise.

Most successful franchisees have built on both positive and negative career experiences to evaluate franchise possibilities and select franchises that best met their professional and personal needs.

Advantages of Franchise Ownership

Safeguards against failure are built into the nature of the franchise itself, and these advantages go far to reduce the risk for the new business owner. Franchises sell nationally known and extensively tested products for which a market has already been established. Many franchise organizations require a well-grounded business and marketing plan from franchise applicants. Applicants must usually submit proof of financial solvency and of sufficient capital to buy the franchise and keep it maintained until it can turn a profit. The parent company may provide assistance and training in choosing a location, setting up shop, estimating potential sales, and designing market strategies that have worked in similar locations.

Cooperative buying power enables the franchise owner to purchase supplies at lower costs from distributors serving all franchises in the chain. Sometimes the parent company helps franchise owners to establish credit, which is an attractive benefit, since a new business usually takes at least six months to become profitable. Often this period is longer; sometimes a business is never profitable. Even franchises of a successful parent company can fail.

Disadvantages of Franchise Ownership

Franchise owners pay a franchising fee plus a percentage of their profits to the parent company. This percentage is determined by the amount of advertising and consulting support given by the parent company and varies considerably. It can range from 3 percent to a whopping 50 percent in some kinds of businesses. The franchise fees are relatively high in the temporary-help business. However, in this business, the franchisor finances the payrolls of the franchisees.

Moreover, the stipulation that the owner must buy both equipment and supplies from vendors specified by the parent company may prevent the franchise owner from making more economical purchases elsewhere.

Before entering into an agreement, a prospective franchisee should read the fine print and get legal advice as well. The law requires that franchisors provide a detailed franchise prospectus to potential franchisees. It is wise to keep in mind that the business of the franchise parent company is selling franchises, and as with all businesses worth their salt, it is going to make the product as appealing as possible.

The potential profits and estimated costs of setting up the franchise that are presented by the parent company should be confirmed by questioning other owners of the company's franchises as well as other objective sources. The Federal Trade Commission requires franchisors to divulge any litigation in which they have been or are involved. Because fraudulent claims and franchise scams have sometimes been pervasive, a franchise agreement should be entered into carefully, with expert legal advice and as much outside knowledge of the parent company as possible.

Growth in Franchises

Continuing growth in small businesses includes franchises. Although mainstream franchises such as hotels, fast-food restaurants, and car-rental agencies have reached a saturation point, new opportunities in business and professional services are available. Manufacturers are franchising specifically defined aspects of the distribution process such as sales territories and delivery routes in order to reduce overhead. More franchise opportunities will be available partially because it costs less for a company to franchise than it did in the past. For example, uniform disclosure documents are accepted in all states, which helps to reduce legal fees.

Home-based franchises may cost only thousands, while the most expensive franchises can cost millions. The percentage of these costs required in cash varies with prevailing credit conditions but usually ranges between 20 and 40 percent when money is tight. The remaining percentage can be bank-financed and pledged with personal guarantees and collateral. Franchise agreements are not to be entered into lightly. The monetary cost of failure can be considerable.

Some failed franchises are bought back by the franchisor or bought by another prospective franchise owner. Franchises fail for many reasons. Lack of financing to support the business until it becomes profitable may cause failure. Even with services and training provided by the franchisor, some owners simply lack the skills required to run a successful business. Often investors buy franchises and hire others to run them. Incentives are different for paid employees versus owners. Thus, lack of involvement by the investor is often cited as the major reason for business failure. Another, and potentially much more serious, problem is that sometimes the parent company fails, causing all franchisees to shut down—successful or not.

SOURCES OF INFORMATION ON FRANCHISES

The growth of franchising can be tracked in *Entrepreneur* magazine. The *Franchise Opportunities Handbook*, published by the Bureau of Industrial Economics and the Minority Business Development Agency of the U.S. Department of Commerce, can be found in the government documents section of most libraries. Published monthly, it carries a list of franchises for sale as well as insightful tips for prospective franchise owners, such as a checklist for evaluating a franchise, information on financial assistance, and a bibliography of sources of franchising information. Online you can access the *Canadian Franchise Directory*, the *U.S.A. Franchise Directory*, and the *Virtual Franchise Expo* by going to globalfranchisenetwork.com. Other sources include the following:

International Franchise Association
1501 K St. NW, Ste. 350
Washington, DC 20005
franchise.org

Which Franchise International
375 W. George St.
Glasgow G2 4LW
United Kingdom
whichfranchise.org
Also has offices in Ireland, South Africa, and the United States.

The sources cited provide information on many franchise opportunities. These franchises should be investigated thoroughly by contacting both the Better Business Bureau and the International Franchise Association. In addition, many excellent books on franchising are on the market, a number of them available through the International Franchise Association itself.

ECONOMIC TRENDS AND THEIR IMPACT ON MARKETING CAREERS

New graduates in 2008 were expected to see a good job market in the marketing field, according to the National Association of Colleges and Employers' *Winter 2008 Report.* In spite of economic uncertainties, average annual beginning salaries for marketing grads were projected to be 5.2 percent higher than in 2007, at $43,459.

Other administrative areas did not receive as large an increase, but engineering and computer technology increases were slightly more.

Changing trends in both the global and U.S. economies are expected to impact the job outlook in the long run. They will most certainly affect the nature of the workplace and job responsibilities as the twenty-first century moves toward the end of its first decade.

Understanding trends in marketing and in the economy is particularly important for entry-level job seekers. Significant transformations in American business over the past ten, twenty, and thirty years have impacted marketing jobs and careers, including the following roster:

- Vastly increasing world population
- Globalization of business
- Outsourcing of U.S. jobs to other countries, especially in manufacturing, certain kinds of technology, and customer service
- Continuing shift from a manufacturing to a service economy
- Continuing shift from privately owned to publicly owned companies

- Deregulation of financial, real estate, banking, insurance, and other key industries, allowing more mergers and acquisitions and the growth of more megacorporations
- Internal restructuring of corporations as middle managers are cut to trim costs
- Impact of computerization and the Internet
- Diversification of the workforce, especially by new immigrants
- Changing lifestyles of American families, with more parents of young children moving into the workforce
- Social, economic, and financial costs of the war economy
- Loss in the value and strength of the U.S. dollar in the world economy

These transformations are major ones, and they affect the types of products being sold, the nature of jobs involved in marketing them, the demand for individuals with certain skills, the salaries offered to workers, and the sizes and locations of the businesses themselves.

Throughout this book, trends related to specific fields have been highlighted, salaries and demand statistics have been cited, and opportunities for individuals in certain areas have been discussed. This chapter presents a broader perspective to help you make realistic comparisons of job opportunities across the field of marketing.

SERVICES MARKETING

We live in a service-oriented economy. According to the Bureau of Labor Statistics, marketing and sales jobs are expected to increase by about 16 percent between 2006 and 2016, and most of these jobs will be in service industries. Less opportunity is expected in marketing jobs in the manufacturing industries, which will likely see negative growth between 2006 and 2016.

In the United States, roughly 75 percent of all jobs are in services industries. Small businesses employ more workers than large ones. New college graduates may encounter some good opportunities in fields that they had never considered or about which they know little. To better understand marketing opportunities in the services industries, it is necessary to differentiate between goods and services from a marketing perspective.

Goods are concrete, physical products produced for specific uses. Examples are computers, cars and trucks, medicines, and clothing. *Services* are activities performed for an individual or an organization. Examples are health care, consulting, and advertising and marketing. While a physical product is impersonal, a service is highly personal. Its quality is contingent on the performance of the worker and can vary considerably from company to company, and even within a company.

Service marketers direct and implement a service firm's marketing effort. Using marketing researchers to determine the needs of the chosen market and the price that customers will pay for the firm's service, service marketers function much like any other marketing manager. Service industries may be equipment based, people based, or a combination of both. For example, electronic databases, automated bank tellers, and diagnostic medical equipment are the tools of equipment-based service industries. An advertising agency is people based; only by motivating and inspiring people can managers assure that the service rendered is premium quality.

Services are intangible. Marketing services is considerably more complex than marketing goods and entails different challenges. Banks and airlines cannot give away samples or claim admirable qualities that will outlast those of the competition. By their nature, services go out of existence almost as fast as they are created and must continually be re-created. They cannot be repossessed if bills are unpaid.

Services cannot be stored as inventory; they must be produced on demand. Long lines or an inability to accommodate customers can seriously impair a service business. Services cannot be mailed; they must be delivered on the spot at a convenient location. Quality is hard to control, and similar services can vary greatly from organization to organization, from employee to employee, and even for the same employee. Everyone has bad days. These unique aspects of services mandate attention and focus by the marketers in a service industry.

The employees are the assets in human-intensive services such as advertising and consulting. Sales representatives who sell services perform the same activities as those selling goods, as portrayed in Chapters 6 and 7. A notable distinction is that service companies gain much of their business through referrals from satisfied customers.

A retail store selling goods might lose some business if a salesperson is rude or incompetent. If it is a specialty store, a customer might return but avoid that particular salesperson. In a service business, on the other hand, the service itself is the product. A customer receiving poor service likely will not return and will communicate the dissatisfaction to others. The success of the service firm depends on hiring the best employees. The pressure to deliver high quality is intense.

Most new college graduates will be employed in service industries. Experts predict continuing high demand for services sales representatives. It is advisable for prospective entrants to identify an industry as well as a field, and to prepare for its unique demands. Areas in which demand will be particularly strong for sales representatives are temporary-help services, business and financial services, information services, and advertising sales. Competition among professional service firms is affecting hiring practices. More of these companies are hiring marketing directors, coordinators, and business development personnel. Responsibilities of professional service marketing include research, coordinating seminars, and writing brochures.

CHANGES IN THE AMERICAN ECONOMY AND BUSINESS

A turbulent period began in American business during the 1980s, causing major restructuring in corporations, much of which continued through the 1990s and into the twenty-first century. A continuing pattern of aggressive acquisitions and buyouts changed many corporate identities and resulted in widespread layoffs and loss of economic health for many small U.S. communities.

Recession and competition from abroad forced additional downsizing and restructuring. By the mid-2000s, recession and the collapse of many corporations in the high-tech industry, the revelation and staggering costs of several major business and financial frauds, the cost of war in Iraq and U.S. military actions and occupations in other countries, climate changes, and the cost of multiple natural disasters, such as devastating storms and the destruction of the city of New Orleans by hurricane and flooding, were all severely stressing the American economy. By 2008, many economists questioned whether a deeper recession lay ahead, and many industries faced hard challenges, including the possibility of more layoffs and deeper restructuring.

Assigning limited resources in a vastly more complex global marketplace is a major challenge confronting most managers today. The business environment of the next decade will be characterized by an uncertain economy, increased global competition, shortened product life cycles, rapid development and marketing of new competing products, and growing demand from customers for better quality, environmental sustainability, and more personal economy and convenience.

Customer relationship management (CRM) has become an essential strategy for corporations that must compete successfully in a much broader and more varied marketplace. Many companies use CRM systems to collect customer data and provide better service.

In the current market, more is being required of every worker, and entry-level jobs will be all the more varied and challenging. Add to this picture the fact that training programs have been curtailed or dropped entirely in some cases as an avoidable expense. Many new employees often must shoulder heftier responsibility on their own. Help-wanted ads regularly feature phrases such as "energetic self-starter," "must be able to hit the ground running," "must be able to work independently," and "must be available for weekend work as needed."

Managers with more work than they can handle are forced to delegate tasks to lower-level and beginning employees. Project teams will be more widely used as companies attempt a more entrepreneurial approach to product development. Some aspects of work will be less structured. More freedom, as a result of reduced numbers of supervisors, will enable newer employees to show what they can do.

Marketing activities result in sales and profit; therefore, marketing will often get the lion's share of the available resources. The downsizing of staffs within different departments will contribute to the trend of outsourcing. Often contracting out certain types of work is more cost effective than maintaining in-house departments and staff for the function. Contracting out advertising, sales promotion, and public relations campaigns will become more common, which is favorable news for the firms dispensing these services. Marketing and economic research and consulting firms also will be positively affected by this trend.

THE IMPACT OF CHANGING TECHNOLOGY

Advances in information and communications technology have revolutionized the workplace and created opportunities for companies and individuals that simply did not exist even ten years ago. Computers are faster, cheaper, smaller, and infinitely more powerful than ever before.

New communications technology has enabled managers to make more decisions, and better-informed decisions, and to make them faster. Sophisticated marketing research analysis such as multivariate statistical analyses, which are extremely complex to perform manually, can be done handily on computers. Monitoring the economic and business environments has been made much simpler through the power of the Internet.

Advances in computerized design and production, as well as in manufacturing equipment, allow managers to respond faster to competition, and improved distribution and inventory techniques make sales campaigns more efficient and effective. Improved graphics technology has led to sweeping changes in the strategies and techniques of the field of advertising.

Breakthroughs in telecommunications technology have furthered the development of branch or satellite offices and the expansion of global operations. In short, technological change has dramatically affected every aspect of marketing.

EFFECTS OF THE INTERNET ECONOMY ON MARKETING

The Internet economy has further globalized the national economy of every country on earth, and it has provided the most explosive growth frontier experienced by advertisers since the advent of television. Many new jobs are expected to result from its continued growth.

We are only beginning to see the results of this technological advance. It will more radically change the economies of developing countries as it puts their citizens in touch with people around the world.

Its political power is linked to its economic power, as we have begun to see in China, India, and Russia. These countries and others have entered more significantly into world commerce and have also experienced some social upheaval in response to the dissemination of knowledge brought about by the relatively open Internet.

CHANGES IN LIFESTYLES AND VALUES

Individual lifestyles and values have been evolving over the years. More and more people are viewing work as a way to maintain lifestyle, rather than developing lifestyles consistent with work. The family is taking center stage in the choices people make, both in their careers and as consumers. People are marrying and having children later in life when both careers are already in place. With an ever-increasing number of two-career couples, both partners share in family responsibilities. Though studies show that women miss work more frequently on days when children are ill, men are sharing this responsibility more often. In addition, the divorce rate has been on the decline. Women with young children often work from home—for other organizations or as proprietors of their own businesses. Information and communications technology enables companies to allow some of their employees to work off-site. Part-time or at-home employment is an attractive option for many workers. It is also being practiced as a cost-saving economy by more and more companies, because in many cases, at-home part-time employees do not get company benefits if they work less than a certain minimum number of hours per week. Also, the company does not have to maintain individual office space for them and therefore saves a second time on overhead.

Contingent workers are self-employed and/or work part-time; this classification includes those who do not work a set forty-hour week, year-round, or for only one employer. It embraces a variety of workers, such as part-time clerks; home-based hairdressers; home based customer service representatives; freelance writers, artists, and photographers; performers such as many actors and musicians; self-employed wedding consultants; babysitters; cleaning people; dog trainers; and academic tutors. Contingent workers make up a sizable percentage of the workforce and allow American businesses a degree of flexibility that they would not otherwise have.

THE JOB MARKET

The job market for marketing professionals is expected to remain healthy and to grow at or above average between 2006 and 2016, with some variation to be seen among individual segments.

In today's market, changing jobs is common as applicants seek enhanced compensation and benefits, challenges, and growth potential. Workers today are managing their careers as businesses, with earnings and profits being given priority. Those with technology skills, especially, are finding that changing jobs and even industries is becoming easier, since companies use similar tools and strategies for competing in the modern global economy.

Some employers are using phased retirement programs, including shorter workweeks, temporary work, or opportunities to work from home, to keep employees longer. Most demand will be for managers and people with mastery over the technology supporting the global economy.

According to the *Occupational Outlook Handbook*, the number of managerial jobs in the areas of marketing, including advertising, public relations, promotions, and sales, will rise by about 12 percent, or as fast as average, between 2006 and 2016—to approximately 590,000 total jobs in the United States.

Overall, the demand for business and management majors has been consistently strong. In the areas of sales and marketing, demand has increased, particularly for business-to-business marketers. Marketing professionals are employed throughout the country and abroad by manufacturers, retailers, advertising agencies, consulting and public relations firms, product testing laboratories, business services firms, government, and nonprofit organizations, among others. Those who have mastered the information technology that connects the customer to all the people in the organization will be greatly in demand.

The aging of America is also rippling the job pool. Though many baby boomers have sufficient financial resources to retire early, they are also healthy enough to work longer. It is unclear what the overall picture will be in the future regarding older people in the workforce. Mentoring of younger employees is expected to become more common, since older managers possess the business acumen needed to run business operations.

In the past, temporary help was usually clerical in nature. Today, contract and temporary-employment agencies can provide a production line for a month or field a complete computer team to conduct a lengthy project. These agencies give employers flexibility and embody more varied opportunities for individuals who want to work independently. The trend of outsourcing by companies is expected to continue, offering independent contractors and consultants new horizons but, at the same time, exporting some marketing-related jobs, such as customer service, to other countries.

Candidates and companies find each other in many ways. Job seekers still use job advertisements in periodicals, but more and more use online job listings. Headhunters and employment agencies are also becoming more plentiful. An increased number of recruiters on college campuses signals an increased demand in some industries and can give new graduates a boost in their job search.

Companies and other organizations are always looking for the most highly qualified candidates, but uncertain economic conditions will impel employers to be more thorough in interviewing and researching candidates' backgrounds and achievements.

TRENDS IN EMPLOYMENT AND COMPENSATION

In the global economy, opportunities in marketing careers exist virtually all over the world in companies of all sizes. However, considerable tradeoffs in terms of quality of life, cost of living, and the merits of the job must all be considered. As expected, salaries in marketing tend to be highest where the cost of living is highest.

In general, larger companies with more than five hundred employees pay higher salaries than smaller ones. In Canada, above-average sales and marketing salaries in every industry are correlated with higher corporate profits. A number of websites provide salary information, including The Salary Center (salary.com).

Business students today have a right to be confident that they will find good jobs even in a slowed economy or recession. Top industry choices include management consulting, investment banking, and e-business consulting.

For new graduates in marketing, salaries can differ by several thousand dollars a year for the same job, depending on geographic area. Salaries for similar work also vary from industry to industry. Since employers within an industry are typically competing for the same workers, industry-wide salaries are somewhat consistent but fluctuate according to the size of the company and the budgets of the specific departments. Within service industries, firms providing engineering and research services usually pay more than other service firms. The National Association of Colleges and Employers surveys job offers to new college graduates. This information can be retrieved from many college career centers or from the Web at nace web.org.

In researching salary figures, it is not unusual to find that different surveys measuring the same thing yield different figures, because the sample groups may differ. The figures reported throughout this book have been used because they are consistent with the overall picture presented in multiple reliable sources, but they, too, should be taken as approximations.

Salary is only part of the compensation picture. In response to employee demands, employers are offering better and more varied benefit packages. Some of the following items, plus numerous others, may be included in the package: health insurance, dental insurance, life insurance, disability insurance, vacation, sick leave, paid holidays, bonuses, pension plans, employee stock ownership and/or stock purchase plans, and profit-sharing plans. Even in a declining economy, *Fortune* magazine's best one hundred companies to work for in 2006 were cited as continuing to offer enticing perks. Of these companies, some provide on-site day care, concierge services, domestic-partner benefits to same-sex couples, fully paid sabbaticals, and bonuses for referring new hires. Job applicants must evaluate the organization's benefit packages to compute and compare total compensation.

Many aspects should be thought through before an individual accepts a position with a firm. Compensation alone is not enough of a basis for making an employment decision. Company training and development opportunities are also meaningful benefits that should be duly evaluated as part of a job offer. Savvy job seekers investigate companies thoroughly and ask probing questions during the job interview.

CHAPTER 12

BEGINNING A SUCCESSFUL CAREER IN MARKETING

Smart new business graduates understand that the likelihood of their early success in a marketing career depends on getting the skills employers seek and landing a good first job. The Internet provides virtually unlimited access to helpful information for accomplishing this goal.

Employers today place skills above everything else when hiring. Preparing for a career in marketing involves acquiring these skills through educational programs and gaining experience through part-time jobs, internships, and participation in campus activities. Many of the best jobs will be in corporations, nonprofits, and colleges and universities. Once prepared to enter the job market, an individual should put a variety of resources to use to hone in on the best possible job opportunities.

GETTING THE BEST EDUCATION

Depending on an individual's professional goals, the required background for a career in marketing may be gained in high school, vocational school, technical school, community college, four-year college, university, or online programs. Educational requirements are discussed throughout this book as part of the specific job descriptions. This chapter supplements that material by explaining where to obtain this needed education and training.

Most of the careers discussed in the foregoing chapters require college and university degrees, and some require graduate study. Probably the most useful source of information on educational programs nationwide is the *College Blue Book*. This five-volume set is particularly useful to people seeking highly specialized programs. The volume entitled *Occupational Education* includes a listing of available programs of study in technical schools and community colleges, organized alphabetically by state or by subject area. Another volume, *Degrees Offered by College and Subject*, features degree programs offered by two-year colleges, four-year colleges, and universities. Other volumes offer narrative descriptions of schools, costs, accreditation, enrollment figures, scholarships, fellowships, grants, loans, and a lot of other information.

The *College Blue Book* is found in the reference section of the library along with many other educational resources. Also available in most college and university libraries is a variety of college catalogs, enabling one to compare curricula of different schools offering the degree or program of interest. Education is an important and expensive undertaking. A person should shop for it the way he or she would for any other item of value. Gaining information from counselors, teachers, local colleges and universities, people in the field, and potential employers is advisable before selecting an educational program.

One important consideration when choosing a program is whether it has national accreditation. National bodies that accredit these schools are the American Association of Collegiate Schools of Business, the Association of Independent Colleges and Schools, the National Association of Trade and Technical Schools, and the National Home Study Council.

GAINING THE NECESSARY EXPERIENCE

As you know by now, experience is required for many of the more desirable marketing careers. This experience can be gained through internships and cooperative programs, part-time jobs, and involvement in campus activities.

Internships and Cooperative Programs

Traditional internships are usually three-month summer positions, while cooperative programs (co-ops) last a college quarter, a semester, or longer. Internships are sometimes coordinated through the pairing of an interested faculty member and a company manager, and the intern is not always paid. Co-ops, on the other hand, are part of an ongoing college program for which students receive both credits and remuneration. These distinctions aren't as clear anymore, however, as companies want interns for longer periods, and they frequently offer paid internships. Many organizations hire their brightest interns and co-op students. As mentioned earlier, professional associations represent a storehouse of information on internships available with member companies. Student membership in some professional associations is available at a reduced cost and is worth investigating.

Internships are advertised on college campuses through placement offices, on billboards, through faculty members, in campus newspapers, and in books such as *Peterson's Internships.* Online sources of internships can be found at sites such as InternshipPrograms.com.

Part-Time Jobs

Apart from intern and co-op programs, many students find part-time jobs on their own that yield both pay and experience. Most part-time jobs available to students are in sales. Though these positions often pay minimum wage and are sometimes hard work, this direct experience carries weight with prospective employers. For one thing, the area of sales is vital to marketing—most activities in marketing are done to maximize sales and profits. Second, employers of part-time students can furnish precious recommendations for full-time jobs. Prospective employers like to hear that a candidate is reliable, works well with customers and coworkers, and has assumed an assistant manager role on occasion.

Many on-campus jobs can be obtained through student financial aid and job placement services. In addition, located throughout every college campus are job boards and student publications advertising openings. Graduate assistantships are available to qualified students. Any opportunity for work experience prior to graduation should be considered because of the strength it lends to the job search for that first, all-important, full-time job.

Involvement in Campus Activities

An option to all students is involvement in campus activities and organizations. By joining student business associations and taking a role in student government, undergraduates can hone the interpersonal skills needed in most marketing professions. Leadership experience in campus organizations is desirable to corporations. Though grade point average and work experience speak volumes, they do not always reveal the potential for leadership. Campus leaders, rather than scholars, are often hired for jobs in many business fields. The charisma that helps students gain elective offices also scores high marks in job interviews. Participation in organized sports, by both men and women, also increases the strength of the person's resume, because learning how to be a good team player is a transferable lesson. Team playing, along with the acceptance that the coach may not always be right but is never wrong, has probably influenced promotion in corporations as much as academic preparation.

DEFINING CAREER OBJECTIVES

Competition is always keen for good jobs, so undergraduates should develop job-finding skills as a part of their education. The first full-time job out of college is particularly important because it sometimes sets the direction for an individual's entire career. The first step in the job search is to decide what attributes you want in the job and how the job fits into your overall career objectives.

Since all individuals do not define a good job in the same way, each job seeker has to define what he or she personally wants in a job before beginning the search. For example, to an entry-level employee, a good job may be one offering growth through a formal training program or company-financed continuing education; to an individual with a disability or to a parent with young children, a good job may be one that can be done in the home; to a student, a good job may be part-time or have flexible working hours; to a partner in a dual-career marriage, a good job may be one available locally; to an ambitious woman, a good job may be one in a company employing women managers in key positions. Again, job seekers should have their individual requirements and career goals clearly in mind prior to launching the job search.

LOCATING JOBS

The task of finding a good job is twofold in that seekers must identify both companies with existing openings and companies for which they would like to work. The fact that a company does not have an advertised opening does not mean that it would not create an opening for an outstanding applicant. This state of affairs makes the job search more complicated, but it also presents the seeker with more promising paths to pursue. Students should build a network of family, friends, and associates who can refer them to others who might be able to help with their careers.

Many experts maintain that the way to find excellent jobs is through direct contact with the person who has the authority to hire. One of the best and most widely read books on the subject of job finding is *What Color Is Your Parachute?* by Richard Nelson Bolles. Although this book is not specifically geared to marketing careers, the strategies for conducting the job search are universal. This book helps job seekers organize their time and energy expenditures and avoid tactics that rarely, if ever, pay off.

Various avenues for locating job opportunities, which are treated in more detail in the following sections, include college placement offices, published job openings, recruiting firms, professional association placement services, job fairs or career days, and online recruitment services.

College Placement Offices. Prospective college graduates should take advantage of on-campus interviews arranged by the college placement office. Surveys of companies indicate that a large percentage of their new college hires come from these interviews. They provide an opportunity for a first contact with representatives of major companies while still on campus. Since these companies are recruiting for current job openings and are willing to hire beginners, young job seekers should definitely avail themselves of these opportunities. It is advantageous to sign up early, because the company representatives have time for only a limited number of sessions.

To prepare for these interviews, individuals should review the respective information on file in the college placement office. This information, provided by the interviewing companies, often includes annual reports and recruitment materials from which students can glean facts about a prospective employer and the career opportunities it offers.

Published Job Openings. Sources of listed job openings in business and marketing include *Career Employment Opportunities Directory*, *Career Visions*, and *Peterson's Job Opportunities for Business and Liberal Arts Graduates*. These references can usually be found in the career planning and placement offices of most colleges and universities. They contain reams of information, including listings of career opportunities, locations of employment, special training programs available with the companies, benefits provided, employer profiles, and addresses to write for further information. *Peterson's* also contains descriptions of the job market as well as tips for job seekers.

Professional journals provide another source of published job openings. Many journals devote a section near the end to advertising job postings. The *New York Times*, *Wall Street Journal*, and other big-city and local newspapers advertise openings, but responding to newspaper advertisements is rarely the route to obtaining good jobs. You will probably find that going directly to the source and writing to the companies for which you would most like to work is the most profitable approach. Newspaper and other job ads can be useful, but you should not feel inhibited about addressing your most desired workplaces directly.

Recruiting Firms. Some job opportunities are listed with recruiting firms. These firms provide needed services to both hiring organizations and applicants. Although it is unusual for a beginner to find a highly desirable job through a recruiting firm, and often a sizable chunk of the first month's salary must be paid, these firms do offer some entry-level jobs that enable beginners to get much-needed experience. When demand is strong, many organizations seeking employees assume the charges for the service.

Professional Association Placement Services. Many professional associations sponsor placement services. A few of the most well-known include the following:

National Association of Colleges and Employers
Public Relations Society of America
Society of Research Administrators
Women in Communications, Inc.

Even trade associations without placement services may provide directories of their members free of charge, or at a minimal cost. Trade associations can often recommend or supply additional sources of information. Numerous professional associations and their addresses are listed throughout this book.

Job Fairs or Career Days. College recruitment conferences are held regularly in large cities around the country. These career conferences enable new graduates to meet employers that do not normally recruit on their campuses.

Many schools and communities also sponsor job fairs, in which company representatives talk about opportunities within their firms. In addition, many offer seminars in job-seeking skills.

Online Recruitment Services. Online recruitment services are gaining in popularity and now number in the thousands. They make both job seekers and companies more accessible and are an efficient way of exchanging information and asking and answering questions. Numerous websites offer thousands of job opportunities.

By 2007, nearly every large organization in the United States, and in every other developed country as well, had set up a sophisticated and informative website. Most publicize job openings, and many also provide a slew of helpful information about applying for work in the organization, especially for new graduates. The big job boards provide listings of a variety of jobs in all areas; job seekers can uncover many possibilities after surfing for a few hours. In addition, candidates can assess their skills, build resumes, research companies, and take part in chat rooms or online classes. Free-agent sites provide a way for freelancers to connect with employers seeking candidates for short-term projects. Auction sites enable applicants to bid for projects or jobs. Niche sites, designed for specialized jobs and skills, are gaining in popularity. For positions in public relations, marketing, and advertising, PRandMarketingJobs.com publishes a weekly e-letter with employment news.

Among the many online employment services, some of the most useful include the following sites:

Monster.com
Computerjobs.com
Guru.com
Vault.com
Eresumes.com
Careerpath.com
Review.com
Hoovers.com

GAINING COMPANY INFORMATION

An individual should always have knowledge about the specific companies with which he or she will be interviewing. It is useful to study the companies' websites and also to check out their background and histories in the reference department in the library. The latter step can be indispensable, since company websites will not often tell you if the company had to suspend operation of a division, or if it laid off a hundred workers a couple years ago. The point is to equip yourself with as much inside scoop as possible, before and after you go for the initial interview. Once you have met the first interviewer and have talked with people at the company, you will have new questions, and a second research effort can yield more insight.

Published Information. Industry information is extremely valuable to the job seeker. Numerous sources of industry information are available. The current *U.S. Industrial Outlook* analyzes approximately two hundred industries, with projections into the future. It is published by the Bureau of Industrial Economics of the U.S. Department of Commerce and can be found in the government documents section of the library.

Job seekers can turn to Standard & Poor's *Industry Surveys* for current and basic analyses of the major domestic industries. The current analysis includes latest industry developments; industry, market, and company statistics; and appraisals of investment outlook. The basic analysis includes prospects for the industry; a review of trends and problems; spotlights on major segments; growth in sales and earnings of leading companies; and other categories over a ten-year span.

Many publishers compile and standardize detailed information at the company level. *Dun & Bradstreet Directories*, *Moody's Manuals*, and *Thomas's Register* all provide specific company information, such as address and phone number, what the business produces, annual sales, and names of officers and directors. For insight into the backgrounds of people who make it to the top in a particular company, researchers can consult *Dun & Bradstreet's Reference Book of Corporate Management* and *Standard & Poor's Register of Corporations, Directors, and Executives*. These resources are shelved in public and college libraries in the reference section. Annual and quarterly corporate reports to stockholders are usually housed in the college career placement offices.

The following directories carry listings for specific areas in marketing:

Standard Directory of Advertising Agencies
Consultants and Consulting Organizations Directory
Dun's Consultants Directory
Franchise Annual
The Sourcebook of Franchise Opportunities
Bradford's Directory of Marketing Research Agencies and Management Consultants in the United States and the World
The Green Book: International Directory of Marketing Research Houses and Services
O'Dwyer's Directory of Public Relations Firms

Online Information. A useful Web location for company information is vault.com, which presents responses from employee surveys across a range of industries. Such inside dope as the interview process and the dress code is covered along with company business and relevant market information. The gleanings here help round out what can be learned from the companies' own websites.

Information on companies can be used by the job seeker to target employers to contact, eliminating companies with low growth potential; to identify a job specialty for the resume; and to compile a list of intelligent questions that will impress any interviewer.

Other Information. Another way to gain information about what is happening in companies in the marketing field is by reading professional journals. Along with advertised openings, these journals provide a wealth of facts to help the job seeker ask timely and well-informed questions during the interview and to make a final decision on what company would be the best employer.

THE RESUME

The first contact that most job seekers have with a company is through the resume. It has to be good, or the applicant may never gain an interview. Remember that you never have a second chance to make a good first impression. Every statement should show how the applicant is qualified for the position in question. As a reflection of one's skill in written communication, it is a perfect way to bias the interviewer on an applicant's behalf before he or she even walks through the door.

A resume is basically a sales device. It should do three things. First, it should emphasize the most positive features in the individual's background, such as maintaining an A average in college. Second, it should stress work experience and positive contributions to former employers. Third, it should describe positive personal attributes and abilities. Individuals write their own best resumes, as opposed to professional resume-preparation services. Only you can present yourself in the best light and sound truthful doing it. That said, it is wise to get some editorial help from a career counselor or other skilled professional, since the resume should make the best possible impression.

Resume Basics

The following are some basic hints for writing a good resume:

- Readers usually skim resumes in the initial screening process. Too many numbers, wordiness, poor spacing, and unclear headings all make a resume difficult to skim. Strongest positive points should be made first.
- No matter how terrific or well experienced a person is, a resume for a new college graduate should not exceed two pages. Job seekers should use more pages only if their experience is sufficient to qualify them for a

management position and/or after excluding all nonessential entries, such as hobbies. It's always preferable to stick to the facts and save philosophy for the interview, if asked about it.

- Unnecessary words such as *I*, *he*, or *she* should be eliminated. Resumes are usually written in phrases—not complete sentences.
- Action words such as *coordinated*, *supervised*, and *developed* should dominate. A resume should be oriented toward results and accomplishments rather than duties. The tone should be as positive as the content.
- The document should be free of spelling and grammatical errors and neatly typed or printed on white or ivory rag paper. No fancy binders, please.
- Salaries, reasons for termination, references, supervisors' names, politics, religion, race, ethnic background, sex, height, weight, and pictures should be excluded.
- An individually typed cover letter should accompany each resume sent to a prospective employer. The letter should be addressed to a specific person whenever possible. In it, applicants introduce themselves, explain the reason for writing, describe potential contributions to the company, and request an interview. A job target should be identified in the cover letter if a target resume is not used.

Copies of all letters sent should be kept in one file folder, responses requiring action by the applicant should be kept in a second, and rejection letters should be kept in a third.

With these basics clearly in mind, the applicant should write a resume that is a summary of his or her skills, education, work experience, interests, career goals, and any other items that qualify that individual for the position sought.

Resume Formats

A choice of formats is available for developing a resume. The preferred format depends on the background of the individual.

Chronological Resumes. A common format is a chronological arrangement of education-related and work experience, each listed separately, with the most recent experience first. If an applicant is seeking a job that is a natural progression from former jobs and has a respectable work history with growth and development, this is a sensible format to use. In contrast, if an applicant's work history consists of part-time jobs while in college, there is a better format—the functional arrangement.

Functional Resumes. A resume organized around functional or topical headings stresses competencies. Such headings as "Research" and "Marketing" enable the job seeker to include course work, special projects, and work experience. These headings are geared to the type of position desired. Actual work experience is included at the bottom of the resume. Both functional and chronological resumes can be used for broad career objectives.

Targeted Resumes. A format used widely today is the targeted resume. Jobs have become more specific and highly defined than they used to be. Beginners who are aware of the job market will have developed some special areas of expertise in order to become viable candidates for some of the best positions. The job target is clearly stated along with specific areas of expertise related to the applicant's ability to do the job.

Which resume format is optimal is a function of the applicant's experience and career objectives. A first-class resume increases the likelihood that the individual will be contacted for an interview. This contact is often by phone, so job seekers should keep a pad and pen beside the phone to record any information from such calls. The more organized and in control an applicant appears, the more impressed prospective employers will be.

Before putting your resume online, or enabling another party to disseminate it, you should be aware of some privacy pitfalls and some things that can be done about them. For a person who is currently employed and wants to change jobs, there is a chance that the present boss will end up receiving or coming across the resume if it is given to a headhunter and is then posted online. One measure that can be taken is to include a legend on the document that forbids headhunters from transmitting it without permission. Before posting your resume to an online site, ask the site administrator whether resumes are traded or sold to other databases, and proceed accordingly. If currently employed, you can also list your qualifications but withhold your name and have inquiries go to an anonymous e-mail account. An alternative to posting your resume online yourself is to register with a job agent service such as CareerBuilder.com, and the site will notify you of job openings.

Some students have also used multimedia technology to create "cyber-portfolios" that contain personalized voice and photo greetings, links to previous employers' Web pages, and displays of college projects and special-interest items.

Recommended books for information on resume writing include *Resumes for Advertising Careers*, *Resumes for College Students and Recent Graduates*, and *Resumes for Sales and Marketing Careers*.

PREPARING FOR THE INTERVIEW

Once you have been granted a date for an interview, it's time to take steps to prepare. It may be possible to obtain a schedule of your visit to the company in advance, including the names and titles of the interviewers. If any are senior managers, their backgrounds could be researched in an industry who's who or another source, and some aspect of this background might be useful to mention during the interview. Job candidates may also request a sample copy of the employee newsletter, relevant company publications, or the most recent annual report to stockholders.

Because applicants usually are allotted some time during the interview process to ask questions, it is best to have a concise list of pertinent questions prepared, some based on the preinterview research. Here are some general examples:

- How are new employees trained and developed?
- What type of performance appraisal system is used?
- How is the company's career development system set up?
- What are some common career paths within the company?
- How long has the prospective supervisor held that position?
- What is the management style of the company?
- In what direction is future growth anticipated?

Any specific information that applicants have been unable to gain in advance that might bear on their career development should be learned in the interview, if possible.

Good grooming and conservative dress—without looking uniformed—is usually the safest bet for a job interview. Women might wear a simply tailored suit, neat hairstyle, understated jewelry, and moderate makeup.

Perfume is not advised, because an interviewer may have an aversion or even be allergic to it. Men might wear a conservative suit, shirt, and tie. Polished shoes, trimmed and styled hair, and neatly manicured fingernails complement the look. Above all, be clean and organized in all respects. In general, opt for the best quality of wardrobe that you have or that you can afford, and keep the style appropriate for the interview environment. Even if you would likely be allowed to wear jeans if you get a job in the art department, wear your best-quality suit for the interview.

Posture sends a message, as do all forms of body language. A firm handshake, good eye contact, poise, relaxed but self-controlled ease, and good manners all contribute to a positive interview. Novice applicants can sometimes measurably improve their overall performance at a job interview by practicing beforehand in front of a mirror.

A portfolio of college experiences might be useful to show to a prospective employer at the interview. This portfolio can include outstanding class papers; descriptions of projects completed for courses, internships, or jobs; and flyers from events in which the student participated or played a role in organizing, such as seminars or fund-raisers. Anything related to the skills needed for the prospective job should be represented.

THE INTERVIEW

Each corporation has a unique corporate culture. An applicant's ability to fit into this culture is often the ticket to being hired.

An applicant can size up the corporate culture during the interview process by unobtrusively observing the employees, as well as the environment, including the lobby, human resources department, work areas, washrooms, lounges, and cafeterias. For example:

- Is there stringent security, or more of a clublike atmosphere?
- Are employees relaxed and friendly with each other?
- Is everyone treated with respect?
- Is there a rigid dress code, or is a variety of style evident?
- Is the coffee served in gold-trimmed corporate mugs? In plastic cups?

- Do the executives pick up their own phones?
- Do employees' workstations display only framed degrees and certificates, or are family photos in evidence as well?

The applicant's ability to discern the operative degree of formality and modify interview behaviors accordingly might make the difference between a job offer and disappointment. The fact is that managers are looking not only for levels of experience but also for types of individuals who would fit comfortably into the organization. In other words, chemistry between candidate and interviewer is nothing to sneeze at. Both parties need to determine whether they would like to work together daily. This is a highly subjective choice.

The applicants most likely to be hired are able communicators on both the professional and personal levels. Marketing graduates have an edge, because most of them know how to sell things—including themselves. They are usually warm, outgoing, enthusiastic, and self-confident by nature.

Keep in mind that typically, both the applicant and the interviewer are under stress. The more relaxed both people can manage to be, the better the interview will proceed and the more information will be exchanged. The interviewer is assessing both substance, which is basically the applicant's past performance and accomplishment, and personal style, which includes communication skills, composure, self-confidence, and motivation.

Broad questions such as "How would you describe yourself?" and "How can you contribute to our organization?" elicit the applicant's values and personality as well as capacity to organize thoughts. How a person fields questions also demonstrates performance under pressure, quickness, energy, and sense of humor.

In general, employers regard specific skills and experience as more relevant qualifications than educational background. Written and oral communication skills, related work experience, and knowledge of the functions of the company are primary assets. This is not to say that grade point average and course work are not scrutinized also. The gist is that most employers care more about what you can do for the company than what you have learned in college, so, in both the resume and the interview, job seekers should accent their skills and how these skills can be leveraged by the company.

Often a member of the human resources department conducts a preliminary interview. This screening helps determine whether the candidate will fit into the corporate culture. If the session goes well, usually the manager of the department in which the applicant would work conducts a second interview. In most cases, an applicant should ask questions as the interview progresses. However, if the interviewer appears formal and conveys a high need for structure, it may be prudent to wait until asked if there are any questions. The applicant's questions should emphasize professional growth and work-related activities. Such topics as salary and benefits should be raised after the job is offered. Some bargaining may then occur, particularly if the applicant has another bid in hand.

The irony here is that most applicants forget to ask for the job. If you are interviewing for a position that you definitely want, then before saying good-bye, you should both state that you would very much like to have the job and thank the interviewer. At the conclusion of the interview, if not before, some indication of when the applicant will hear from the company is usually given.

Unfortunately, the interest that an interviewer shows in an applicant does not necessarily translate into a job offer. Displaying interest and polite warmth is standard operating procedure in the business; the interviewer is building goodwill and keeping the applicant invested. Applicants should go on as many interviews as possible and carefully compare companies and offers, no matter how well a first interview unfolds or how certain an applicant is that an offer will be tendered. Additional offers will provide the advantage of choice and will also give some leverage to the applicant, who can then bargain more strategically for salary and benefits.

Each person is his or her own best resource. By using sound judgment in choosing and planning a career, studying information gathered from a variety of sources, and relying on well-formulated questions as well as self-knowledge in accepting a job, you can multiply your chances of success in a marketing career.

ABOUT THE AUTHORS

Lila Stair is a professional author in the areas of careers and business. She holds an M.A. in counseling from the University of New Orleans and an M.B.A. from Florida State University. As an instructor of business courses at both the community college and university levels, she has had the opportunity to teach business concepts and to assist students in selecting business careers. As a former career counselor, Lila Stair has worked with hundreds of students, counseling and providing them with career information, and she has also worked with employers in job development and placement.

Leslie Stair studied business and communications at Tulane University, in New Orleans, and served as secretary of the Alpha Kappa Psi business fraternity. Working on the professional committee for the fraternity, she arranged speakers for the group, learning from these professionals the importance of such areas as internships, networking, resume development, and interviewing skills. An internship at the Charles W. Schwab branch in Tallahassee, Florida, allowed her to experience the power of computers and information firsthand in marketing financial services.